GOODWOOD
·DRESSAGE·
CHAMPIONS

GOODWOOD
·*DRESSAGE*·
CHAMPIONS

JANE KIDD

Foreword by
THE DUKE OF RICHMOND & GORDON

Kenilworth Press

First published in Great Britain 1994 by
The Kenilworth Press Limited
Addington
Buckingham MK18 2JR

British Library Cataloguing in Publication Data
A catalogue record for this book is available from the British Library

ISBN 1-872082-56-4

Design by Paul Saunders
Typeset in Linotype Goudy Old Style 11.5/15
Typesetting and layout by The Kenilworth Press Ltd
Printed and bound in Portugal by Printer Portuguesa Lda

CONTENTS

꧁꧂

The Duke and Duchess of Richmond and Gordon.

Foreword by
THE DUKE OF RICHMOND AND GORDON

❧❧❧

FIRST, on behalf of my wife and myself, I would like to say how much pleasure we have received from running dressage events at Goodwood over the last twenty-one years. By that I do not just mean watching beautiful horses being superbly ridden, but getting to know personally so many dressage riders, judges and supporters, both British and foreign.

It has been a privilege to be involved with the development of dressage in Britain at a time when the standards of dressage in this country have been rising so rapidly, and it is most rewarding for us to think that these events at Goodwood have played some part in this improvement.

Many people regret the closure of Goodwood as a centre for dressage events, but there was virtually no alternative. First it had become impossible, due in part to the recession, to find the very considerable sum in sponsorship money which the international championships required. Furthermore, my wife and I ran the events with much personal involvement and attention, and having moved out of Goodwood House, this would no longer have been possible for us. In addition our son, Lord March and his wife, who have moved into Goodwood House, although they ride, are not involved in dressage.

Finally, there are some particular people I would like to thank: Margaret Winn for having acted as dressage secretary for twenty years; Jane Kidd for writing this book, as well as *Festival of Dressage*, and many articles on Goodwood in *Horse and Hound* and elsewhere; Diana Mason, for most of these years chairman of the British Horse Society Dressage Group, and the late Jean Sansome, secretary of the Group, for their support and encouragement; Tilly Pot and her husband, Jaap, for enlivening the international event for twenty consecutive years, and Wolfgang Niggli and his wife Madeleine, for twelve years the chairman of the FEI Dressage Committee, for encouraging us to introduce many innovations; the many voluntary helpers, stewards, judges, writers, runners and others for their loyalty and commitment. Lastly, I want to thank my wife, who brought dressage to Goodwood, and who sustained it with her enthusiasm and hard work for twenty-one years.

PREFACE

GOODWOOD'S EXTRAORDINARY contribution to the horse world and dressage in particular has been fascinating to research. Finding out what turned riders into Goodwood Champions has been a wonderful task for a dressage aficionado like myself.

These top riders have been willing to be interviewed because of the high esteem in which they hold Goodwood, and they wanted to make a contribution to ensure that the role of this stately home and the Richmond family in the growth of dressage can be appreciated and remembered.

I have had some very good discussions and my aim has been to let the riders talk about what has been important to them and not to analyse or comment on their approaches.

There have been some surprising links between these champions, like their early starts in a sport which has been thought of as being for the older riders. Dominique d'Esmé won her first Prix St Georges at nine years of age, Anky van Grunsven started training her first Olympic partner when she was just twelve, Pia Laus was only one year older, Dr Reiner Klimke was winning classes (Prix St Georges) at European Championships when he was only a teenager and Christilot Boylen was seventeen when she first went to the Olympics.

A feature of all their horses is a strong personality and it is amongst the horses that there have been the most dramatic changes over the twenty-one years of Goodwood. The swing towards the lighter type and the huge resources going into selective breeding of horses for dressage has done much to raise standards generally.

Goals are similar but methods of getting there do differ. At a time when arguments rage about the effects of training horses deep and low, many of the champions have expressed their views on the value of this new approach.

There have been changes over the twenty-one years that Goodwood staged international events. When Goodwood started, the arenas were grass and quite hard, and it was not unusual, even in Continental Europe, to compete on such surfaces. Today, horses rarely venture off soft surfaces, where there is little jarring and it is easier to

maintain and develop key factors in today's dressage – elasticity, roundness and the natural nobility of the horse.

With more horses being bred with the natural ability for dressage, better conditions for training and competing, and the highlighting of the artistic element through the music freestyle, during the years of the Goodwod Internationals dressage standards have risen generally and the competitions are easier for the general public to appreciate. I have been lucky to have had the chance to record these developments.

ACKNOWLEDGEMENTS

Many more people than I can mention have helped in putting this book together, but invaluable contributions have come from the Duke and Duchess of Richmond and Gordon, Margaret Winn, Peter Willett, Major Anderson, Rod Fabricus, Jennifer Stobart, Patrick Daniels, Nicholas Williams, Wolfgang Niggli, and of course all the Champions.

Some of the books that have helped me are: *Lord Paramount of the Turf*, Michael Seth Smith (Faber & Faber); *Records of the Old Charlton Hunt*, Earl of March (Elkin Matthews); *Goodwood's Oak*, M. M. Reese (Threshold); *Goodwood Racecourse Media Guide*; *Goodwood*, David Hunn (Davis Poynter); *The Correspondence of the Dukes of Richmond and Newcastle 1724-1750*, Timothy J. McCann (Sussex Record Society).

PHOTO CREDITS

Jim Bennett – 134; John Birt – 18 (bottom), 49, 52, 62, 68, 70, 72, 84 (left), 99, 104, 120, 127, 138, 141, 142, 145, 146, 158, 160 (left); John Bunting – endpapers, 34, 77, 107, 112, 114, 116, 124, 153; Iain Burns – 71, 119, 137, 144, 147; Hugo Czerny – 44, 53, 54, 56, 57, 59, 61, 93, 96, 102; John Elliot – 30; Werner Ernst – 48, 64 (right), 83 (top), 94, 110, 113, 125; Sue Feast – 160 (right); Elizabeth Furth – 51, 81, 83 (bottom), 84 (right), 87, 100, 108, 148, 156, 158; Kit Houghton – 24, 33, 38, 89, 155; Leslie Lane – 37, 150; Bob Langrish – 40, 43, 67, 128, 139; Trevor Meeks, courtesy *Horse and Hound* – 69, 82, 132; Jacob Melissen – 129; Stuart Newsham – 121; Desmond O'Neill – 90; Sally Anne Thompson – 60, 64 (left); Trustees of the Goodwood Collection, 6, 12, 15, 17, 18 (top), 21

INTRODUCTION
Goodwood's Contribution to the Horse World

ON THE WESTERN edge of the South Downs, overlooking the cathedral city of Chichester and its harbour of sparkling grey sea, lies some of the most glorious land in England. These Downs, parks and woods have been the site for an extraordinarily large number of significant developments in the equestrian world, thanks to the patronage, energy and vision of the Richmond family who own the Goodwood estate. Horses are in their blood as they are direct, if illegitimate, descendants of Charles II, the king who played a major role in the development of flat-racing, the establishment of Newmarket as the headquarters of British racing and the creation of the Thoroughbred, the fastest and most valuable breed of horse in the world.

FOXHUNTING

Charles II created his natural son by Louise de Quéroualle, Duke of Richmond, and, with little stigma attached to illegitimacy, took him into the Court and spoilt him openly. They both shared a love of the horse and at ten years of age the young Duke was riding in races at Newmarket, and at eleven, he was appointed Master of the Horse. At thirteen his father died, and the young Duke's security evaporated as there were fears that he might claim the throne. He was forced into exile with his mother, became a Catholic, but then reverted to the Church of England faith when William III inherited the throne and allowed them back to England. It was a turbulent upbringing and it ruined his character. Good-looking, intelligent and able, he became wayward, a gambler and an extravagant spender, but he still enjoyed his sport.

At the time, the new-found 'fun' for the English aristocracy was foxhunting in Sussex. Until the late seventeenth century, the fox had been hunted only occasionally when the nobler beast, the stag, or the cleverer one, the hare was not available. The fox had been thought of as cunning, and therefore it demeaned the aristocracy to chase him, but attitudes changed when it was discovered that his speed and wily ways provided a more exhilarating chase for those who were keen riders. The open downs and the woodland coverts around Goodwood were ideal country over which to pursue the fox.

Charles Lennox, the first Duke of Richmond, son of Charles II and Louise de Quéroualle, by Wissing.

It was one of the first Duke's half-brothers, the Duke of Monmouth (the eldest illegitimate son of Charles II), who discovered that the downs behind Chichester were such a great place for foxhunting, and he had the stature to encourage the noblest in the land to try this alternative to staghunting. It was the time to do so, as this form of hunting, traditionally the sport of the nobility, was facing problems. The country for staghunting, namely the forests and parks, was disappearing in the wake of the agrarian revolution that had brought the land under cultivation. In addition, poachers were killing more deer, helped by the increasing availability of firearms. Other quarry were being sought and although some took to the hare, the fox ran faster and was more exciting, if not so subtle, to chase. It is possible that the fox had been hunted on the hills north of Goodwood for centuries, but it took the Duke of Monmouth to make the area famous for foxhunting. When in their turn the Richmonds took over the hunt, their contribution was to turn it into a well-organised, formal activity.

It was natural that the first Duke, being such a good rider, should try out the sport for himself, and he was so entranced that in 1697, at twenty-three years of age, he paid £4,100 to acquire Goodwood for use as a hunting lodge.

The centre of the hunting activities lay two miles north of Goodwood in the tiny hamlet of Charlton, after which the hunt was named. This small village was invaded by the nobility of the land. Even King William III came down, as did the Duke of Devonshire, the Earl of Halifax, General Compton, and countless other titled gentlemen.

At first it was Monmouth and Lord Grey who owned a pack of foxhounds each, with Mr Roper, a great expert on hounds, managing them. With Monmouth's demise after his ill-fated attempt to seize the Crown in 1685, the Duke of Bolton (his son-in-law) took over the hounds, and when he in his turn gave up hunting because he fell in love with an actress who preferred London life, the second Duke of Richmond took them over as Master of Foxhounds.

He was thought to have been born in that Jacobean hunting lodge at Goodwood. He grew up to hunt, and it became a central interest of his life, with him taking over this, the most famous mastership in the country when he was twenty-seven. Over the following twenty years he helped make it not merely the most important hunt in the country but also one if not *the* major social sporting occasion with the nobility invading that tiny village of Charlton. Taking as an example a meet in 1743, seventeen peers and their retainers, and their 143 horses moved in. Richmond encouraged the nobility to participate and he ensured its continuing high stature by turning the hunt into a formal society with rigorous requirements for membership.

The second Duke was such an avid foxhunter that he liked to start at eight in the morning. However, he found the two-mile trek from Goodwood to Charlton to be rather long for these early meets. So, when he had a windfall on the gambling tables he used his winnings to build Foxhall, a hunting lodge in Charlton itself, with stables for 140 horses.

On a hunting morning a hundred or more horses would be led out of Richmond's stables, the grooms and hunt servants wearing the distinctive livery of blue with gold cord around the edges. They often had great sport, but the most famous hunt of them all took place in January 1738 when the hounds ran for ten hours, covered fifty-seven miles, and the hunt ended at 5.50pm with just twenty-three hounds and three riders – Billy Ives, the Duke of Richmond and General Hawley.

Although hunting was the second Duke's passion, and he will always be remembered for his formalisation of the sport of foxhunting, he did get involved in many other activities, such as being a patron of Canaletto, becoming Grand Master of the Freemasons of the Grand Lodge of England in 1724, becoming a General and defending the King in a battle with the Jacobites.

Hunting cost the Duke about £1,000 a year, but he was much more prudent than his father and built up a sizeable income. A considerable boost to this was his marriage settlement. Allegedly his father arranged his marriage to Sarah, daughter of the Earl of Cadogan, when she was just thirteen years old and he seventeen in order to settle a gambling debt. It took place in The Hague in 1719 and the young Earl of March (he had not yet assumed the title Duke of Richmond) was not pleased about this being forced upon him and made a rapid departure on the Grand Tour of Europe. Three years later on returning to London he was so reluctant to meet his wife again that he chose to go first to the theatre rather than to his home. There he was captivated by a beautiful young woman who was the toast of London, and was much surprised to discover that she was his wife Lady March. It was a romantic start to a very happy twenty-eight-year-long marriage producing twelve children. The marriage settlement helped them buy Singleton and Charlton farms, amounting to 1,200 acres. Good management of the funds helped towards many improvements to the estate, including building a menagerie for a collection of strange animals and planting unusual trees such as the cork oaks and cedars of Lebanon.

Horses still played a part in the second Duke's highest roles as he too was appointed Master of the Horse, in 1735. This important position also gave him a place on the privy council, and although he carried out his duties so effectively that he was the longest serving Master of the entire century and kept the office until his death in 1750, it was said to be very hard to get him to London during the hunting season.

His son, the third Duke, also a keen foxhunter, took over the Mastership but had a rather different attitude towards the sport and changed both the name of the hunt, from Charlton to Goodwood, and the nature, from a series of important social occasions that brought the nobility out of London to a more local event with the majority of the followers coming from the area. This made the foundations more solid and reliable, but ended those heady days when the villages were invaded by the most famous in the land.

The third Duke was the greatest of the Richmonds, leaving a huge inheritance of property, land and works of art which became the basis of the current family's treasures. As a free-thinker who said at seventeen: 'I prize liberty beyond anything,' he made some important contributions to the country's development. He created the Ordnance Survey, sponsored and trained the Royal Horse Artillery and stood up to the government to support the American Colonist's call to be able to control their own taxes and defence.

When the British government decided after the Boston Tea Party to put forward a bill to suppress coastal trading, Richmond said at the second reading: 'I say the present bill is cruel, oppressive and tyrannic. I contend that the resistance made by the colonists is in consequence of other acts equally cruel, oppressive and tyrannic. Such a resistance is neither treason nor rebellion but is perfectly justifiable in every possible and moral sense.' After this outspoken statement he did not attend the third reading, which being presented in December probably clashed with a hunting party.

He also did much for the country's culture, returning from a three-year long Grand Tour laden with treasures that were not to be solely confined to the gaze of his family and nobility. In 1758 he set up a small academy in his London house where people who could not afford the Grand Tour could look at and study the work of foreign artists and craftsmen. This preceded the opening of the Royal Academy by ten years.

His patronage of major artists at an early stage in their career was another important contribution. He recognised the exceptional talent of the barely known Liverpool artist George Stubbs and invited him in 1759 for a nine-month stay. The Duke's patronage of this most famous of all equestrian artists was given before Stubbs' book, *The Anatomy of the Horse*, was published in 1766 and before he worked for many of England's nobility, including the Royal Family. In the catalogue to George Stubbs' exhibition at the Tate Gallery in 1984 it is stated, 'After Stubbs arrived in London in 1758, the first commission of considerable importance that he received was from the Duke of Richmond, which obliged him to go and reside at Goodwood. During those months at Goodwood he painted his first mature pictures, including the 'Study of Horses Exercising' and other hunting scenes, and a few years later was commanding higher prices than Reynolds, who incidentally painted no less than seven portraits of the third Duchess.'

Today the Stubbs works hang next to some of John Wootton's paintings of the Goodwood Hunt. The Wootton depictions pre-date the Stubbs paintings by twenty years, being from the time of the second Duke, and they show distinctly that the quality of the hunters had improved.

The third Duke's approach to hunting was different from his father's. He must have been a more sensitive person, ahead of his times (he did, after all, submit a bill for universal manhood suffrage 138 years before it was achieved). He demanded fair play for the foxes, not allowing any 'view holloa' to assist the hounds, so that followers had to wait for the sound of the horn and the hounds to know when the fox had broken covert. And if a fox went into his earth the huntsman was ordered to whip off the hounds.

He thought so much of his animals that when he moved the hunt to Goodwood he built hunt kennels that were architecturally superior to the house. James Wyatt was the architect, and he designed huge rooms for the hounds, complete with a seventeenth-century form of central-heating. M.M.Reese in *Goodwood's Oak (The Life and Times of the Third Duke of Richmond, Lennox and Aubigny)* said, 'The hounds of the Charlton Hunt were more comfortable than the Duke's guests.'

The third Duke of Richmond, by Batoni.

He took equally good care of his horses, employing William Chambers (architect of Somerset House) to design the stables for his hunters. Their accommodation was so palatial that they dwarfed the main house, both in regard to quality and size. This was later corrected in respect of size because Wyatt went on to design, but never complete, a new octagonal house, but it is still generally recognised that in terms of quality the horses had more distinguished residences than their human masters. It was symptomatic of the Richmonds' relationship with the horse world that their animals were given such sumptuous dwellings.

The third Duke had a very happy marriage but his wife was not able to give him any heirs. There were illegitimate children, and one even lived at Goodwood, but the title went to his nephew, who inherited a large estate, wonderful works of art and a famous foxhunt but many debts. The fourth Duke needed to be and was prudent. He decided to dispose of his foxhounds, but it is not clear whether this was done to economise, or whether, when he took over as Lord Lieutenant of Ireland, he realised he was not going to be at Goodwood enough to make running a pack realistic. He gave the hounds to the Prince Regent and nearly a century of great hunting over the Goodwood estate came to an end. By this time, however, foxhunting had become an established sport in Britain with its centre, as it is today, being Melton Mowbray and the Shire counties. Goodwood had shown the way but was now removing itself from the scene. Ironically the hounds did not last long when taken from those luxury kennels: they developed rabies symptoms and had to be put down. Even more ironic was the demise of the fourth Duke: he was appointed Governor General of the British Settlements in Canada in 1878, and whilst there the bite of a fox led to his death through the same dreaded rabies. He had tried to separate a dog, probably his, from a fight with a fox and a tiny, lethal scratch was his reward.

Hunting was not, however, finished at Goodwood. The sixth Duke was a horseman of considerable skills. He won many flat-races including, in 1842, five races at Goodwood's July race-meeting. He helped his son, the Earl of March, to revive the pack and the future seventh Duke became its Master. There was tremendous excitement on Monday 5th November 1883 when the first meet of the newly formed hunt with fifty-five couple of hounds was held. It was a wonderfully colourful sight with the gentlemen of the hunt in those famous blue coats and the huntsmen and whips in the Lennox livery of yellow coats with scarlet collars and cuffs. The Master and his followers accounted for thirty-four horses and, in all, about two hundred people found some sort of horse or pony to ride. This auspicious occasion brought back a flavour of the past and the reason why the Richmonds had come to Goodwood.

They had orchestrated the revival in style, hiring the most famous huntsman in the south of England, George Champion of the Southdown hunt, whose descendants are still leading huntsmen today. In the past, three hundred square miles of country had been available for hunting, but times had changed. Farming was in the midst of a disastrous depression, with cheap grains from the USA flooding the market. Landowners could not afford to have their land damaged, so more and more closed their farms to the hunt. The conditions were no longer similar to those that had made the area famous two hundred years before, and in 1895 the Duke gave up the unequal struggle and closed the hunt.

RACING

It was the third Duke who started the sport for which Goodwood became just as famous as it did for foxhunting. There was a good stretch of wonderful downland turf known as the Harroways where the stands now lie, down to the hill that led towards Charlton. This had long been used for informal races, and in April 1800 the third Duke ran some more organised events for the officers of the Sussex militia. These were such a success that the Duke determined to lay a proper track and to run a two-day meeting under Jockey Club rules in 1801. This time there was much more of a sense of occasion, with tents to house the many spectators and a ball in the evening in Chichester to lure the less horsey and more social types to the races.

The *Sporting Magazine* recorded the event thus: 'The company was splendid and numerous, and, for the accommodation and refreshment of whom, by order of the Duke of Richmond, five or six roomy tents were pitched, in each of which collations, consisting of every dainty in season, were profusely served up.'

The racing itself bore little resemblance to today's with the Thoroughbreds being

The third Duke of Richmond and his brother with the Charlton Hunt, by George Stubbs.

much smaller, tougher and more substantial. It was stamina and strength, not speed, that were required for the conditions of these races. The first race, for instance, was a Hunter's Plate with two-mile heats. Traditionally there were three heats, each with a half-hour break between them so that the horses could be rubbed down and taken down to the start. The winner was the horse that won two out of those three gruelling heats. The jockeys were also pretty different – this Hunter's Plate was confined to gentlemen riders who had to carry seventeen stone. Other races did not demand so much weight-carrying capacity as there was one for horses carrying ten stone, but the amateur spirit was still a feature as the mounts had to be the property of gentlemen who had hunted with the Duke of Richmond's hounds.

The success of this two-day meeting led to even further expansion next year, with the innovative and energetic Duke, despite his severe gout and advancing years, organising a meeting at the end of April over three days. A wooden grandstand was constructed and the whole event turned into a great social occasion with balls, theatre parties and opportunities for the local families to entertain. The Prince of Wales attended as did the Duke of Norfolk, the Lords Egremont and Chichester, and one of the most exciting races must have been the match for 100 guineas when the Prince of Wales's Rebel beat the Duke of Richmond's Cedar.

The 1803 April meeting suffered from the weather that can be so cruel at that time of year, and the war with Napoleon must have taken away some of the gentlemen riders and spectators. The attendance was down, but there was no decline in the social events which were associated with the meeting and which had become a feature of it – balls, parties and the theatre. The Duke of Richmond with his generous hospitality and

The kennels (TOP), stables (LEFT), and grooms' and huntsman's houses (RIGHT).

The courtyard inside the stables at Goodwood House.

vitality had established a new type of race meeting; Glorious Goodwood had become part of the social scene, and one that has endured to the present day – although after the disaster of the April weather the dates were changed to July.

Large funds had been needed to support the ventures for which the third Duke will be remembered – the race meetings, the house and stables, and the works of art. His nephew, the fourth Duke, was more sensible and cut back on many of the excesses including the racing. This was also due to him not being able to spend much time at Goodwood. He was an eminent soldier and accompanied his friend the Duke of Wellington through the Battle of Waterloo. It was, however, during his time as the Duke of Richmond that one of the most famous Goodwood races was started: the Goodwood Cup. This was a three-mile race that became one of the most prestigious of all British races following the victories in it in 1831 and 1832 of the great Derby winner Priam. Another famous winner was the top mare Kincsem, winner of all her fifty-four races. She had come all the way from Hungary to beat the British horses in 1878. Then, in 1884, arguably the greatest racehorse of all time, St Simon, won this race by twenty lengths. The Goodwood Cup was the great stayers' race, with only the Ascot Gold Cup being its equal. It is questionable that the fourth Duke played much part in its instigation for it was his son who was the real racing enthusiast and he had his own first win in 1818 with a horse called Roncesvailles. His greatest success, however, was in 1827 when his horse Linkboy won the Goodwood Cup, a gold trophy which can still be seen in the dining room at Goodwood House. It was the fifth Duke who turned the Goodwood meeting into one that truly warranted that title of 'Glorious Goodwood'.

The fifth Duke was a great and daring horseman, so fearless that he did what was thought to be impossible and galloped down the steep Bow Hill close to Goodwood. He succeeded, but when trying a similar feat down another hill the horse fell and so severely aggravated the near-fatal injuries he had incurred in the Battle of Orthez, that even he did not dare hunt again.

In the army he had been Aide-de-camp to his father's great friend the Duke of Wellington, and as a civilian he was a distinguished politician who became Postmaster General when Earl Grey was the Premier, but horses were a great passion and, no longer able to ride, he directed his energy into establishing race meetings that were the envy of the country.

He found a great partner in these projects, Lord George Bentinck, the second son of the Duke of Portland. Like the Duke, Bentinck was a politician and a horse lover who also won a race at Goodwood, in 1824. Bentinck was a natural and very strong leader who was dubbed 'Dictator of the Turf'. The fifth Duke had another asset as his father had rationalised the Goodwood estate and his mother had inherited the Gordon estates in Scotland, turning him into the fourth largest landowner in the country with 300,000 acres.

Racing at Goodwood set such an example that the national administrators had to follow suit. Racing had long provided villains with an infinite range of opportunities to make money, but Richmond and Bentinck determined to make it a clean sport in which all racegoers would be well treated and could expect to make bets with the confidence that the racing was fair. They started by providing efficient management of those Goodwood race meetings, took account of general racegoers, giving them better facilities than at other courses, and introduced such established aspects of today's scene as the pre-race parade and an unsaddling enclosure. The starter was given a flag instead of having to rely on his voice to shout 'Go', the Clerk of the Course was fined if races started late, and horses had to wear a number that corresponded to both the racecard and the one on the number board.

In all of these ventures there were no committees, which helped the pair put through their projects much more quickly and effectively. Apart from cleaning up their racing at Goodwood, and thereby setting a standard which the Jockey Club had to follow, they also improved the facilities and provided for top-class racing. To help achieve this they literally sliced off the top of the Downs and then brought in huge quantities of earth so that the finishing straight could be wider and longer by two furlongs. Prize money was provided to attract the best horses, and famous races were inaugurated, such as, in 1840, the Stewards Cup, which was the first major sprint handicap and has remained a great race to the present day. Another great race started that year was the Nassau Stakes, named such because of the friendship between the fifth Duke and the Dutch royal family, the House of Orange and Nassau.

A new stand was built in 1830 to hold three thousand people, with refreshment rooms, retiring rooms, betting rooms and a glass-fronted saloon. The fifth Duke laid on even more lavish and extensive entertainments than were provided in his great uncle's day. The aristocracy flooded out of London for the July meeting and King William IV's horses filled the first three places in the 1830 Goodwood Gold Cup. Through the 1830s the course was developed further to become, by the 1840s, the highlight of the British racing season. The Bentinck/Richmond partnership provided good clean sport, race conditions and facilities that attracted the top horses, and at the same time made it socially a great occasion. That glorious natural setting was used to maximum effect.

In the newspaper reports about that three-day annual race meeting through the 1830s and '40s there are eulogies about how close to perfection it all was, and the phrase which is still used today, 'Glorious Goodwood', was coined.

Alongside the development of this model race meeting was the conversion of those magnificent stables from use by hunters to use by racehorses. John Kent was hired as trainer and he (to be followed in due course by his son) did so well, that this trio of Bentinck, Richmond and Kent became one of the most influential in the history of racing.

They soon made a name for their ingenuity. In 1836 they had a particularly good horse in their stables called Elis who was second in the Goodwood Cup and won two other races at the July meeting. There was much media interest as he looked a good candidate for the St Leger. When, however, he was still at home in his Goodwood stables four days before the Doncaster race, nobody laid any further bets on his success, as it was too short a time for him to walk there (the only form of transport for horses in those days). When he did arrive at the start of the St Leger looking fit an healthy there was

Goodwood Races 1844, a scene in the park.

astonishment, but he had travelled to the course in 'a stable on wheels', the first-ever horsebox, and Bentinck made £12,000 from the bookies. This financial success for Bentinck was also a significant moment for racing as it enabled horses to race all over England, thus making it a national rather than a local sport.

The Goodwood training centre's heydays were in the early 1840s by which time John Kent Junior at twenty-three was playing a major role, and Bentinck had moved his entire string into the stables, which meant that at times there were more than 120 horses in training. Just as little expense was spared in turning the race meeting into the most famous in England, so was there big expenditure on the training. New gallops were laid at Halnaker, and six inches of mould plus trees on either side meant that frost could not stop the training. As it was three or four miles from the stables to these gallops, bracken was laid on tracks to them so that the horses had a safe route.

The results were amazing with the stables winning thirteen races at the 1844 Goodwood meeting, and eighty-two across the country, including for Richmond the Oaks with Refraction and the 1000 Guineas with Pic Nic. No training establishment had ever enjoyed such a monopoly over the sport.

Lord George Bentinck had achieved practically everything except winning the Derby, and 1846, with more and more of his time being devoted to his work as a politician, in the middle of the Goodwood meeting he announced that his 208 horses were for sale for £10,000. Edward Lloyd Mostyn paid over the sum to acquire the best stud and racing stables in England, but soon found the expenses so great that he sold them. Most, including the colt Surplice, went to Lord Clifden in 1847, and this was the horse bred by Bentinck that achieved his long-held dream of winning the 1848 Derby.

With Lord George Bentinck's departure from the racing scene some of the colour went out of racing at Goodwood, and in 1854, Richmond, after fifty years as an owner, called it a day. Soon those magnificent stables were to revert to their original purpose – to house hunters and visiting racehorses. But it had been a glorious era, and once again Goodwood had shown the way by being innovative and setting new standards for an equestrian sport.

Goodwood's July meeting continued to be a feature in the British racing calender both for the socialites and the racehorses. The Prince of Wales, later King Edward VII, was a great supporter of the meeting and dubbed it 'a garden party with racing tacked on'. Over the last twenty-five years further innovations have been introduced which have expanded its role as a racecourse. That garden party atmosphere and sense of elitism might still be a feature of the July meeting, but the Goodwood Board under the ninth and tenth Dukes have once again been leaders in adapting to the times. Goodwood still attracts the snobs but it has also done much to make racing more attractive to the general public and has broadened the base of its appeal with theme days, children's enclosures and better public enclosures. Goodwood was also the first British course to give live commentaries of the races over the public address system. This was introduced in 1952, largely due to the forward-thinking Clerk of the Course at the time, Ralph Hubbard.

Goodwood has built three new stands original in design and splendid in effect. The first, the March Stand was opened by the Queen in 1980. Another won a commendation from the Royal Fine Arts Commission. Then in 1989 and 1990 the Charlton Stand and Sussex Stands were opened respectively with the latter's stunning roof design being a reason for the four design awards it won.

Goodwood has updated the races making its meeting much more competitive and attracting the top horses. Foremost amongst these is the Sussex Stakes which many consider the most important race in Europe over one mile for horses of all ages.

They have not stuck to tradition unnecessarily, and have changed the day of their top race, the Stewards Cup, from a Tuesday, which it had been on for 152 years, to a Saturday. This is a great boost to the weekend crowd and increases the betting take throughout the country.

Some of the most far-reaching changes have been to the volume of racing, as instead of the one-off four day July meeting there are now eighteen days of racing from May to October, including five days in July. This has changed the relationship of Goodwood to the British flat-racing scene. It is the evening meetings that have been the most original. The Levy Board funded the first but Goodwood increased the number with no support from the Levy board but simply in response to the need of the industry. Known as Enterprise Evening Meetings they were the first to rely on private funding since racing became so dependent on the Horserace Betting Levy Board. Goodwood now runs four through June. This adventurous move has been hugely popular with both the public and the racing industry, and although the evening meetings make little profit they have been recognised as an important service to the sport and to the local community.

The Dukes of Richmond have done much more than ensure that Goodwood racing kept apace with the times. Particularly in the 1980s and 1990s, with Rod Fabricus as

Clerk of the Course, it has once again been a racecourse which has set fashions and standards that others have followed.

HORSE TRIALS

When the ninth Duke of Richmond handed over the running of the estate to his son and heir in 1969 there was a flurry of activity, with part of the house being demolished to make it more manageable and the remainder being redecorated. The future tenth Duke had an unusual mixture of education having been in the army, qualified as an accountant, and studied theology at William Temple College before going on to be Director of Industrial Studies there. It qualified him well for running the estate in an imaginative and commercial manner.

It was, however, his wife, Susan March, who led him and Goodwood in a new direction towards equestrian competitions other than racing. 'When I got to Goodwood I felt I could not live here and not ride,' and so it all started. First there were the horse trials that benefited from blanket coverage of novice events by Midland Bank sponsorship. A novice horse trials in 1971 was the first important equestrian competition at Goodwood, and it went from strength to strength.

With Air Chief Marshal Sir Thomas Prickett, a Goodwood director, as organiser, there was not another horse trial to rival its efficiency, and of course the venue was glorious. The top names in the sport came there and it was such a popular venue that Goodwood was asked to hold the National Championships in 1975 and again in 1976. No less than 186 of the most famous riders in horse trials made that trip to Goodwood for the first weekend in October. The Championship was then moved on to a more central location, to Locko Park in Derbyshire, but Goodwood continued to run an annual horse trials until 1982.

DRIVING

Driving trials also seized the opportunity to hold events in this historic park, under the management of the Earl and Countess of March who were both keen to promote equestrian activities. The first event was staged there in 1976, and it was such a success that they made it the venue for the 1977 National Carriage Driving Championships. It was a new name in driving, local contractor Alwyn Holder, who took the national title for teams, but closest to him were the Queen's bay geldings driven by her husband, HRH the Duke of Edinburgh.

After this, driving, like the horse trials, moved north for the next year's National Championships. However, the Countess of March had been smitten by the sport and she went on to drive her daughter Lady Louisa Gordon Lennox's show pony to be placed in the National Championships. Later she drove a Dales Stallion and then a pair of Welsh ponies.

DRESSAGE

Competitors and organisers loved the ambience of Goodwood, and amongst those who had realised its potential during the horse trials were international dressage judge Sheila Inderwick, and Peter Hodgson, who in the beginnings of dressage and horse trials was executive officer to the two disciplines. They both knew that the Countess of March's interest in dressage was growing.

She explained: 'My father bought me a lovely Thoroughbred and when I was riding him I kept on thinking there must be more to it than this, and then years later I saw Podhajsky ride Little Model and I immediately realised that dressage was what I was looking for all that time back with my Thoroughbred. It is amazing that I had not known it existed.

'When I got to Goodwood I bought an Arab, Sword of Islam, and took him for dressage lessons with Esme Jack. I enjoyed it so much we put on small riding club competitions and ran several dressage courses taken by the Spanish Riding School's Herr Rochowansky.'

It was all beginning to snowball in the direction of dressage, especially when Sheila Inderwick brought to tea at Goodwood one of Britain's Olympic riders, Domini Lawrence (now Morgan). Domini had become increasingly conscious of the debt the British owed the Continentals. British international riders went to competitions on the mainland and enjoyed their hospitality, but never offered them an opportunity to

The international arena in front of Goodwood House, before 1987 when the hurricane uprooted the famous oak on the right.

compete in Britain. Concerned about this, Domini sought support for a British international show and it was Sheila Inderwick who asked Domini to come and sell her idea to some friends. Those friends turned out to be the Earl and Countess of March, and Domini sold her idea over tea but 'on condition that I would get some Germans to come. I had to guarantee that four riders would turn up.' Domini more than fulfilled her side of the bargain for it was not just German riders that turned up but, thanks to support from Georg and Inge Theodorescu with whom she trained, some of the best of the rest came to boost the start of a concept that was to change the face of dressage in Britain.

The timing was good as it was 1973 and it coincided with the opening of a new Goodwood equestrian centre, providing the base for promoting this new development in Goodwood's equestrian history. An indoor school had been built, buildings converted to provide accommodation, and Jennifer Stobart BHSI hired to run yet another form of equestrian activity amongst those wonderful historic facilities designed for hunters and racehorses.

The enthusiasm was enormous, and the visitors and their horses were given wonderful hospitality, but the actual competition facilities were a far cry from those of later years. Not only were there no sand arenas, but the grass ones, although picturesquely situated in front of the house, were on a slope. There were no grandstands, just straw bales for seats. Nor was there much prize money as the Grand Prix was worth a mere £75, the sponsors Sothebys putting up just £353 for three classes.

Nevertheless the Germans sent some of their top combinations with Georg and Inge Theodorescu in action, along with Karin Schlüter on Liostro, but it was the young and barely known professional, Herbert Rehbein, who earned the honour of being the first Dressage Champion of Goodwood. The British were represented in the top classes by Molly Sivewright on Morning Star, Domini Lawrence on San Fernando and the redoubtable seventy-one-year-old Lorna Johnstone on El Farruco.

It was, however, in the less advanced classes that the seeds of the future were planted. British entries in the elementaries included Jennie Loriston-Clarke with Dutch Courage, and in the mediums, Diana Mason with Special Edition (British Olympic team 1976) and Tricia Gardiner with Manifesto (British team Alternative Olympics 1980). Also amongst those competitors in the National classes was the President of the show herself, the Countess of March. She was riding the horse who was the cause of dressage coming to Goodwood in the first place, the grey Arab, Sword of Islam. 'The dressage was all Sword's fault. I did not know anything about it before he came along.' She showed, too, that she did not know too much about competing as she rode in the grass arena without putting studs in her horse's shoes to stop him slipping, and the judge, the number one British trainer of the time, Robert Hall, reprimanded her afterwards.

There was only one foreign judge and that was the late Jaap Pot from the Netherlands. Over the following decade Jaap probably did more than any other judge to help educate the British about the culture and ways of dressage. He also adjudicated at every single Goodwood meeting over twenty years until his untimely death.

This was very much the story of Goodwood. Many of those helpers at that first

Goodwood International were still there twenty-one years later. The Earl and Countess built up a loyal and enthusiastic band of supporters to assist them in their equestrian enterprises: Denis Colton and David Braham as stewards, Millie Collet as scorer, Patrick Daniels as announcer were some of the stalwarts, but none more so than Margaret Winn. She had been show secretary to that very first horse trials in 1971. She transferred to the dressage in 1974 and remained as a superb secretary for every single following show.

In its twentieth-century history, it is towards dressage that Goodwood has made its most notable contribution, transforming a sport that has been considered a rather eso-teric activity, a 'foreign' pastime that did not fit in with the British tradition to ride their horses fast and over fences. Few spectators or riders were interested in it but today it has nearly as many followers as horse trials, it has become a major sport. Events from Hickstead to the Horse of the Year Show want to include dressage in their schedules, because it is a sport in which there has been a huge growth in public interest. Dressage has at last become an activity in which British riders are good enough to win interna-tional medals and the development of the artistic element to the sound of music (a Goodwood inspiration) has given it much more public appeal. With the changing attitudes of the nineties, where harmony, grace and the unity of horse and rider rise above technical competence, dressage has become a sport of the times. It is generally recognised that in Britain the single most important reason for this transformation has been dressage at Goodwood.

THE
GOODWOOD CHAMPIONS

CHRISTOPHER BARTLE

꒰ᜌ꒱ꜞ꒰ᜌ꒱ꜞ꒰ᜌ꒱

CHRISTOPHER BARTLE won for Britain the 1986 Goodwood Championship and became the only champion to ride a non-Warmblood. His partner Wily Trout is an Irish seven-eighths Thoroughbred and this breeding is not the only unusual feature about the pair.

Christopher Bartle was only twenty-four years of age when he gave up three-day eventing to focus on dressage, having before this been a steeplechase jockey. It transformed the image of dressage riders to have a young man brave enough for these pastimes taking up dressage and progressing so well that he earned Britain's highest-ever placing at an Olympic Games (sixth in Los Angeles) and in the World Cup (second in 1987). This was something of a shock for the British, most of whom thought of dressage as a rather sissy activity. Christopher's background and successes were instrumental in changing English attitudes towards the sport.

Wily Trout was an unconventional dressage horse, but then Christopher had bought him to event. 'I had been drawn to the advertisement in the *Horse and Hound* which said he was bold. When he did come into dressage that boldness was a problem in the early days. He tried too hard, but eventually it was a great asset in that he always put everything into his performance. It was one of the reasons for his longevity. He was a workaholic.'

Wily Trout did not, however, have a natural quality trot, which is the one pace that everybody looks for in a dressage horse. 'He had a poor trot, but that is the pace you can improve most and the real value of dressage is to enhance and develop the paces of the horse. I had to work hard on improving the trot.' Amazingly, this lack of a natural cadenced and spectacular trot was not a handicap when it came to the piaffe and passage. Wily Trout had probably one of the best piaffes in his generation of international horses. 'I learnt from him that the piaffe and passage are not necessarily inhibited by a horse not having an impressive trot. It is more the ability to collect and to develop the physique and musculature to support the piaffe and passage.'

True to his Thoroughbred breeding he did have a very good walk and correct canter. 'For me, what made him special was the canter. The flying changes were only a problem

An extended trot from Wily Trout and Chris Bartle. Despite this Irish three-quarter-bred's lack of a natural cadenced trot, his trainability and athleticism enabled him to produce this type of movement.

in getting him confident and relaxed. He had such a correct canter, even when doing one-times. He had a genuine three beat with a big moment of suspension. Often horses become more lateral in their canter in the changes. No matter how collected he was, his canter remained correct.'

The reason Wily Trout ended up in the Bartle family's stables at Markington in Yorkshire was not because of this good canter or even the walk; they did not choose him because they took him through a careful selection process but because the person who tried him before 'said he was nuts and the owner allowed me to have him on trial. I did not see him until he came out of the box looking like a shaggy dog, and it was one of my most dramatic moments when I clipped him out and saw his head. It was love at first sight. There was something about the look in his eye that appealed. I am a great believer in making judgements about a horse from the way they look at you, and look at the world.'

Wily Trout did help Christopher in his eventing ambitions and in 1976 qualified for and was making the final preparations to go to Burghley when he injured a tendon. Their trainer, Baron Hans Blixen-Finecke, who had himself won the Olympic individual gold medal in eventing in 1952, 'was instrumental in making me do dressage with him. In the early days Hans had just thought of him as a lunatic event horse but then he realised he had talent and he persuaded me not to go back to eventing when the tendon healed. But it took me a year to consolidate the changes without him running away.'

In 1978 they made their debut in the Prix St Georges at the Selection Trials. Nobody took much notice as Wily Trout was too excited to settle and do good work, but one of their next competitions was a friendly international, a CDA. There, with Jaap Pott from Holland judging, they finished second to the Dutch visitors Annemarie Sanders-Keijzer and Amon.

This so impressed the selectors that despite having only started in two Prix St Georges, they were invited to compete in the Prix St Georges at the 1978 World Championships at Goodwood. It was their big break, but also their big disaster. Afterwards, Wily Trout, being such a sensitive and intelligent horse, 'never showed his best performance at Goodwood. That arena was always a light-up experience.' At first it all went according to plan: 'He had settled pretty well, and I had worked him thoroughly on the day before, but I had forgotten that the last time he had heard loudspeakers was at his last three-day event in 1976. The Prix St Georges was the first class. I worked him then brought him out for the test. The speakers started and Wily Trout's eyes rolled and the sweat poured out of his skin. He thought the cross-country was about to start. It was a dressage disaster and we ended up second to last.' What a way to make an international debut, but the reassuring factor for all who have had an horrendous test is that Wily Trout went on to be a Goodwood Champion, and the only one lower than him was another future star, the World Cup winner Kyra Kyrklund, who was making her debut at a senior FEI Championship.

The test might have been awful but Goodwood was a source of inspiration to Chris. For that weekend of the World Championships, he had no other class to compete in, and was able to work his horse amongst the greats of the dressage world. The show had also been important to him and his sister Jane's dressage career the year before. 'At that stage I had never seen international dressage or any tests above Prix St Georges. My sister Jane and I went along fully expecting to see something unobtainable. What was encouraging was not so much the magical performances of Klimke and Mehmed but the number of horses that made mistakes and parts of their work that were less than good. It made dressage look possible for us, and encouraging that our horses at home could do as well or better in some of the movements. It was a turning point in our careers.' That Goodwood visit led to the Bartles setting their sights on being successful in dressage, and this is just what they did, becoming the only brother and sister to compete in the same team at the Olympics.

That 'blow up' in that first test at Goodwood did more than damage morale, it was the start of Wily Trout's reputation as being talented but unreliable and tense. 'It seemed no matter how calm I got him it was impossible to persuade the judges and the selectors that he was calm and reliable.' It was the reason they were left out of the British team for the Small Tour classes at the 1980 Festival, but 'that made me more deter-mined and I was placed and best of the British riders. There is nothing that encourages a competitor more than cocking a snook at the selectors!' It probably helped with the selectors, as the following year he was made a member of the senior British team for the 1981 European Championships.

It did not help so much with the judges and that tiresome reputation remained. 'In order to achieve that reliability I had to work him far more than was really necessary to overcome his stage fright. We had to produce below-par performances that judges and selectors could think of as being the reverse of tense. Until they could see a rider working they always thought of it as tactful riding. I received those dreaded words "tactfully ridden" on the test sheet so often, even when I knew he had actually gone well, although there were times when it was true.'

The problem was more than Wily Trout being a high-spirited, bold, sensitive horse, as Chris' philosophy was based on nurturing this eagerness to go forward in response to aids that could not be seen. 'My main underlying aim in any dressage performance when watching or riding is a feeling that the horse is offering something because the rider points him in the right direction and allows it to happen. A performance is marred if there is an appearance of the rider in some way carrying the horse with his hands or legs. The whole appearance should be of the horse showing off, being pleased to be there. This is probably more important to me than anything else. Some horses, because they have a naturally big trot, are always going to be marked well even if the rider is hanging on or the performance does not look easy. This is not what I want for my dressage. I look at the whole, the horse and the rider and the lightness and ease of their performance together.'

This freshness of performance is best developed if the horse has a more general training and his work is not too specialised or confined to work on movements in an indoor school. 'We need to look at the purpose of dressage and go back to its roots. The aim is the harmonious development of the physique and carrying ability that makes the horse a pleasant ride. Part of that physical development comes back to cantering and jumping and both of these keep their minds fresher. Emile Faurie is a good example of that. His work with Virtu has paid attention to that aspect. It is more than drilling them. He has been single minded and brave to stick to his guns. It is easy to get a feeling that you are under pressure to do the movements over and over again, and that is the way to make them better.'

For Christopher, this need to focus on the overall development of the horses and to keep their attitudes alert used to mean 'putting every horse through the eventing routine. But every horse has to be taken individually. Some of the Warmbloods are more confident in an environment they are used to and are happy to work consistently in an arena. Today, I am not hard and fast on an event horse's training.'

He is hard and fast on a 'thinking man's' approach to training, and despite his background as a steeplechase jockey, assistant racehorse trainer and three-day event rider, says he is not a 'seat-of-the-pants rider'. The major reason for this was his mother's influence. Belgian-born Nicole Bartle was 'instrumental in cultivating our interest in dressage and because of her Continental background had an academic approach to

Wily Trout was most famous for his piaffe and this is the movement he is showing off for the last time at Goodwood on his retirement parade at the 1987 European Championships.

riding, and in the training of horses desired to understand the nuts and bolts of it. The art of communication was important.

'I learnt to ride correctly and she got me to understand rather than making me do it.

'It led on naturally to a good relationship with Hans [Blixen-Finecke] as his whole philosophy on training was based on firstly understanding and secondly educating and developing the horse's ability. He coped with schooling problems in an analytical way rather than a confrontational one. That has stuck with me ever since.'

This refined approach to riding was further developed in his gap year between school and university when he went to France and trained with the former *Écuyer en Chef* of the Cadre Noir, Commandant de Parisot. When at Bristol University, however, he gained experience of a more traditional, British approach to riding for at the stables where he rode he was 'put on all the rough old horses from Leicester Sales'. After this he went on to race and event and this mixture of horsemanship was, he believes, helpful to his dressage: 'Especially the racing, as it gave me a sound understanding and feeling of a genuine canter or gallop. The eventing and racing helped me appreciate what it meant to have a horse going forward, to willingly take you forward without being driven. Some riders who come to dressage without that background do not have that natural feeling for when a horse is genuinely forward.

'They helped in other aspects such as balance, and when it came to the flying

Wily Trout and Chris Bartle enjoying that athletic canter, having just won one of their many prizes at Goodwood.

changes it was easier to keep the rhythm and have a feeling for the right moment to give the aids.'

These more sporting types of equestrian activity were helpful in spheres other than the riding. 'I carried over into dressage, thinking of the horse as an athlete in terms of conditioning him muscularly and aerobically and from the point of view of planning a campaign for competitions. It is important to treat the dressage horse like a racehorse in the build-up to important competitions so they peak at the right moment.'

This approach is not so easy today: 'There are so many competitions it is difficult to know when you want your horse to peak. In addition you have the demand from the public for demonstrations and displays. There is a danger of exploiting the horse too much.'

Christopher found this out the hard way, for having followed careful campaigns for getting Wily Trout to his peak for the big competition he forsook it when tempted to take part in the first World Cup with its winter season. At the 1985 European Championships most were surprised that he finished only fourth individually, and there was pretty universal belief that he was unlucky not to earn an individual medal. But this misfortune generated plenty of sympathy and was the start of a very successful run. He was the first British rider to win a World Cup qualifier, in Rotterdam in 1985, one of the first to win an international Grand Prix with a victory in Brussels, and the first to win a Grand Prix Special with a victory in Zuidlaren, then he filled the runner-up position in the World Cup, and took the Goodwood Championship. 'From the World Cup we went straight to the Selection Trials and started the build-up to the World Championships. He [Wily Trout] was in need of a rest and could not have one. Then because he did not go so well at the World Championships he was seen to be a spent force.'

Wily Trout was eighteen in 1987 but still finished second in the Final Selection Trial. Nevertheless he was left out of the team and he went to Goodwood for the 1987 European Championships, not as a member of the British team but for his retirement parade.

Sadly for Britain, Christopher Bartle did not find another partner to keep him in international dressage. 'It is important to me to feel that I have achieved something that I have not achieved before.' He has not found a more talented horse than Wily Trout and as 'I left eventing prematurely there were various mountains I wanted to climb in that sport before age caught up with me.' He has had his rides around Badminton and Burghley, ridden internationally and become the sport's team dressage coach. He has climbed most of those mountains, and his eyes are turning towards dressage again.

HARRY BOLDT

H ARRY BOLDT is one of the most respected names in the history of international dressage. For twenty years was the 'full-back' of the German team, earning twenty-four medals at Olympic Games, European and World Championships, including more individual silver medals than any other rider. Sadly the individual supreme honour always just eluded him.

Upon his retirement he was awarded the top training job in Germany, that of national coach, and under his guidance the country has increased her extraordinary domination of competitive dressage. The winning margins for the team medals have grown larger, and the individual honours have become progressively more and more of a monopoly for his country. At the 1992 Olympics he was a major factor in the incredible German achievement of winning the team gold and making a clean sweep in the individual contest, taking the gold, silver and bronze. Nor is it just as a team coach that he has excelled, for since 1988 he has trained the Olympic quadruple gold medallists, the greatest partnership of our time and arguably in history, Nicole Uphoff-Becker and Rembrandt.

Britain, too, has benefited from his special gifts: in 1993 he started to help the team and was such a major contributor towards their winning of the silver medal in the European Championships that he was elected *Dressage Magazine's* Trainer of the Year.

His memories of Goodwood are mixed. Champion there in 1976 he has also participated as coach to the German team when they had the narrowest victory in recent times, taking the 1987 European Team Championships by just 174 points. He came too with the Verden Auction young Hanoverian horses, who demonstrated to the British the way of going in the early years of training. But his most vivid memories are of the 1978 World Championships. He came to England then as the only rider with realistic hopes of tumbling the reigning European and Olympic Champion Christine Stückelberger and Granat. He had been runner-up to her, earning silver medals at both the 1976 Olympics and the 1975 and 1977 European Championships, and this was his big opportunity. Late in the morning of the Sunday when the individual championship was held he looked over the door of those wonderful Goodwood stables at the greatest

Cosima, the mare that Harry Boldt rode to victory at the 1976 Goodwood International championships.

horse he had ever ridden, Woyceck. True to his placid nature, he was lying down, fast asleep, but disturbed by his master he started to rise. 'Suddenly the hind legs slipped and he fell onto the right hind. When he got up he was really lame. We walked him all the time until I got on. I thought I might have won that individual but with this problem he was only fifth.'

That problem went on and Woyceck never really recovered from that unlucky slip in one of the most distinguished stables in the world, and he was intermittently unlevel for the rest of his career. It is one of the few sad memories of Goodwood, but Harry Boldt had plenty of good ones.

He only came there in 1976 because 'we had heard in Germany that it was famous. It pleased the riders and they said I must go to Goodwood'. He found out for himself: 'It is a good place for dressage. It is always nice to have a big house in the background and a lot of space. The stables are very good. There are really good facilities for horses.'

His partner for that 1976 Championship was the twelve-year-old brown mare Cosima, the only mare in Goodwood's Grand Prix and one of the very few competing at such high levels. It was perhaps an indicator of the style of the time that very few mares excelled. In the 1950s and 1960s there were plenty of top mares like Venetia and

Antoinette (Dr Josef Neckermann), Doublette (Willi Schultheiss) and Tyra (Willi Schultheiss). In the 1990s more and more are to be found at the top levels, but between there were few. One must surmise that as it was a time when there was more emphasis on strong riding to gymnasticise the horse, than on lightness and fluency, this did not suit the mares. Harry Boldt stood out as a quiet rider who put as much emphasis on fluency as on brilliance and this, with his tactful style of riding, enabled him to get along with the sex that was out of fashion as international competitors in the 1970s and 1980s.

Cosima was one of a string of horses that Harry Boldt won on internationally. Son of the dressage rider and instructor Heinrich Boldt, he was trained by him and according to German principles from the beginning.

Harry Boldt expresses this clearly in his great dressage book, *Das Dressur Pferd*, saying, 'Through all dressage training up to and including Grand Prix is drawn a golden thread known as the "scales of dressage training": *Takt* (rhythm), *Losgelassenheit* (suppleness), *Anlehnung* (contact), *Schwung* (impulsion), *Geraderichten* (straightness) and *Versammlung* (collection).'

Harry Boldt's best horse, Woyceck, performs an excellent extended trot at the 1978 World Championships.

His first successful Grand Prix horse was Brokat on whom he was third in both the 1955 and 1956 German Dressage Derby and was placed ninety-five times in S level dressage. His first star was Remus, by the great Anglo-Arab Ramzes, and with him he earned the individual silver and team gold at the 1964 Olympics, the same two medals at the 1966 World Championships, 1963 and 1965 European Championships, and the gold and bronze at the 1967 Europeans.

Golo IV earned him yet another team gold at the 1974 World Championships, where he was also placed fourth individually, but his greatest partner was his last one, Woyceck. A Hanoverian by Wunsh II by Wohler, this powerful horse was ridden by Olaf Peterson's wife Barbara. They made their debut in Grand Prix in Dortmund in March 1975 when Woyceck was just nine years old. Harry Boldt, watching from the ground, was impressed and in the happy position of having a sponsor who would buy him a horse. Hans and Uta Denecke were hobby breeders who were interested in getting involved in dressage. They were lucky as their money bought them a great horse – Woyceck – that could be ridden by a great rider – Harry Boldt. They were unlucky with their timing, though, for in most periods this pair would have been unbeatable but they met Granat and Christine Stückelberger in their prime. Harry Boldt commented, 'For me, my best horse in my life came at the same time as that great horse Granat.' He compared their abilities. 'We were very good at pirouettes and good at all the movements, but maybe not at passage like Granat, and his transitions were very good.'

Woyceck had very special assets. 'Every day he was the same. He was a horse that you did not have to worry what mood he was in. He never spooked. He worked like an engine and was always better in competition than in the warming up. He knew the days when he had to go his best.'

Woyceck and Boldt were an immediate partnership. They were selected for the 1975 German team and for the first time filled that runner-up position behind Granat. They did the same at the Olympics, and then in 1977 at the Europeans at St Gallen they did a great test in the individual ride-off. Granat made mistakes but still came out on top: 'I was disappointed I did not win the gold in St Gallen. Granat did not give Christine Stückelberger such a good ride.'

With three individual silvers on Woyceck and four more on Remus, Harry Boldt came to the 1978 Goodwood World Championships determined to break that jinx. *Horse and Hound's* dressage correspondent, the late Anthony Crossley, tipped him to win, saying, 'In the writer's opinion, favourite for the individual gold will be that fine rider Harry Boldt on his famous and giant Hanoverian Woyceck.' His horse was at his prime at twelve years of age, and although he did break the run on the silver medals, sadly it was in the wrong way, for Woyceck was never the same after that unfortunate slip in his stable, even though he came sound for the 1979 Europeans to win the team gold and individual bronze. Harry Boldt did have one really good ride in 1980 in his home town, and he won and startled everybody by jumping off and saying, 'That is my last test. Woyceck and I have retired. I will never have a better horse than Woyceck.'

Harry Boldt was fifty years of age; he knew what he wanted to do and it did not take

Harry Boldt says that today's horses have the elegance of the Thoroughbred and move like Warmbloods. Rembrandt, ridden by Nicole Uphoff-Becker, is the epitome of this; he has plenty of Thoroughbred blood in his veins and the scope for extended trots like this one.

him long to achieve it. In 1981 he went to the European Championships in his new role as coach to the German team. 'Even in my last years in the team I was learning about it. We had had two coaches, Stecken and Schultheiss. I had watched what they did, listened to what they said and learnt. When I was in the team after each of the championships we discussed what we thought about the training and the coaching.'

His learning was good because he is now the longest-serving German team coach.

He has two different roles, one as coach to the team and one as trainer for two of the top riders, Klaus Balkenhohl and Nicole Uphoff-Becker. 'The home trainers often want to do too much. I have to watch that the horses are not overtrained. I visit the riders at their homes and many times I can tell them if there is a problem. I have had a lot of experience as a rider – for thirty years I rode many horses. When I see problems with a horse I can remember a horse which had the same problem and know what to do. Sometimes it is so simple. The rider cannot believe it is so easy to put right.'

Watching Boldt at work, very little appears to go on. The rider keeps working and then suddenly he asks for a little correction, a small change which alters the whole picture. Because of his ability the riders trust him and have every confidence to try whatever he asks them.

Harry Boldt first came to England as advisor in 1983 when Kalman de Jurenak brought over a collection of three- to six-year-old Hanoverian horses that were being trained in preparation for the Verden Auction. By this time the British had seen plenty of top-class international riders at Goodwood, but this was at the top of the tree, they had not seen them on the way up, they had not seen how the young horses worked, the way of going that was needed to become a good international horse. The Duchess of Richmond and myself were organising national shows at Goodwood at that time and thought a visit by these younger horses could help educate the enthusiastic British riders who were starved of the opportunity to watch horses at this crucial stage. Harry Boldt came with them to add weight to the opportunity for education.

He made some very perceptive observations after watching the normal British dressage riders. He pointed out that dressage was a new sphere for the British and that it was good to see so many riders trying it but that they had been brought up to hunt, event and show jump. The problem for them was that it takes time to learn dressage.

'They cannot change from the other sports and the next year be dressage riders. It takes at least ten years for riders to get a feel of what it is about. It has to be progressive learning. Some use spurs and double bridles but this is not the answer because the seat is not there to make the horse go from behind. To develop a seat, the only possibility is to ride without stirrups.

'The whole idea of dressage has come too quickly in England. You need a broader base on which to build. This base is trainers, and you lack them in Britain. But as the sport develops then the trainers must automatically come along.'

Those ten years have now passed, and he was right. In that time Britain has developed a dressage culture; there are now more trainers, and riders have a clearer concept of the objectives.

Other things have changed in the close-on forty years that Harry Boldt has been participating in top-level dressage. Styles have altered but he believes this has been dictated by the type of horse that is the favourite at any one time. They are now elegant, more Thoroughbred in type. Today they have the elegance of the Thoroughbred and move like a Warmblood. Granat and Woyceck were heavier with very good movement.'

CHRISTILOT BOYLEN

CHRISTILOT BOYLEN was the last Goodwood Champion, in 1993. A quiet, determined and highly focused personality she has had a remarkable career. At just seventeen she rode in her first Olympics after obtaining special permission to break the rules as the minimum age was – and still is – eighteen. She then went on to ride at six further Games, a record which no other rider is likely to challenge.

Although a natural planner, paying attention to every detail, she recognises her lucky breaks. The first was that her Thoroughbred failed-racehorse was a dangerous jumper who dangled his legs and kept turning over when she took him eventing. Her mother, fearful of a terrible accident, wanted to divert her daughter into safer areas and sought out a trainer to help her with some dressage. Germany's great rider/trainer Willi Schultheiss was in need of a break after a bout of tuberculosis and readily accepted a spell in Canada. Of all the trainers, he was the one with a special affinity for Thoroughbreds, most of his great horses being of this breed, and the result was that Christilot found herself cantering down the centre line at the 1964 Tokyo Olympics on her tall gangly Thoroughbred and at an age when few had even thought of trying dressage.

Bonheur had his strong points – a good passage and some good canter work – but like most Thoroughbreds who are bred to gallop not to collect, he found the piaffe difficult. Also, although possessing an abundance of energy this was too often the result of tension which made it difficult to ride a test. Nevertheless, he was good enough to take her to yet one more Olympics in Mexico and she had to wait for thirty years until she found her best horse, her Goodwood Champion, Biraldo. He had plenty of Thoroughbred blood in his veins as both his grandsires were racehorses, but with some more common blood too he had an exceptionally good attitude in the arena. 'He is a great show horse because he gets better the more he knows the routine. Over the years he has been very steady in the ring. The problems have been in the warm-up. He gets nervous at specific items.

OPPOSITE: *Biraldo shows off his extended trot at Goodwood during the last Championships at this stately home.*

Biraldo, showing a great capacity to take the weight backwards onto his hindquarters in a pirouette.

'He has three brilliant basic gaits, and he is not really weak in any area. He has great extensions, excellent piaffe and passage and my only concern is to ride him at the right tempo. He has a great extended walk, but the collected you have to be careful with. His high points are the tempi changes and extensions. You put it altogether and you have a quality horse with a lot of charisma.'

Like most top riders she has clear ideas of her ideal horse for dressage which is one with the three features: 'pureness of the paces, lightness and quickness to the aids, and intelligence.' In the case of Biraldo it was the second which was the weakest, as he was rather unresponsive to the aids, but it is also the one which is easier to fix with good training. 'No horse is perfect, there will always be problems; but the important thing is that the problems are those that you, as a rider, are good at fixing,' and Christilot is good at training a horse to be light and responsive.

She pointed out too that learning to ride and train was only one aspect of being successful. Another was getting good enough horses, and unless the rider is very rich this means work on public relations, and being good at dealing with owners. 'I am an artist at grabbing rides.' The only Olympic horse she owned was her first, and since then she has ridden for others.

Biraldo came into her stables in Germany on trial for a young rider. He was just seven years old, 'fed up with the world and not good in the mouth, but there was an occasional spurt that made me realise there was much more underneath than one thought.' When the young rider did not buy him Christilot worked out a deal with his owner to compete him herself, but with the objective of selling him.

After a season in the Small Tour she was amazed when her trainer, Udo Lange, urged her to try the Grand Prix, but he was right for Biraldo won the three Grands Prix he entered, an exceptional feat in Germany especially considering he was only a seven-year-old. 'I knew I had a major horse who loved the piaffe and passage. He was good enough to shoot for the Olympics.' He did remarkably well for such a young horse, reaching the ride-off and twelfth place, but she added, 'Barcelona came a year too early for us.' In the competitions through the autumn Christilot realised he was making great improvements but was disappointed that the judges were not recognising it and that the marks stayed the same. But then came Goodwood. She was expecting to get better placings 'but that it came so drastically, so suddenly, was a surprise to us.'

As always, there was a detailed preparation for the event. 'The worst thing is to hit the ring feeling unprepared.' Christilot had been to Goodwood before for the 1980 Festival of Dressage. She knew that the arena was special. 'I had great respect for the ring. It was wide open and not set in entirely level surroundings. The horses could gaze way into the yonder. Every show and ring has its own atmosphere. You have to be aware of it and it influences which horses I take and the way I train them for it.'

Biraldo was prepared in their outdoor arena in Germany for the 'wide open spaces' of Goodwood. Then the journey was planned carefully with Sven Rothenberger, who lives close to her in Germany and who shared the transport. 'A successful show starts with planning the travelling and the timing of the journey and the arrival.'

Christilot places great importance on routine, and before the Goodwood Grand Prix she kept to the same pattern of work she always uses for him.' I took him for a walk in the morning. Jogged him long enough to find out how high he was that day (it is a little bit weather based). If there are high winds and it's cold then I test to see how much work he will need to settle him. At Goodwood the wind and rain we had on arrival was over and I planned the usual forty minutes' work before a class.

'For the first fifteen minutes I worked on the stretching and going forward then started on the gymnastic lessons, bending, stop-starts and shoulder-in, building up his attention level, getting him focused, and then started to fine tune the quickness of his reactions. To be brilliant in a test he has to be fine tuned. I use exercises like several steps of shoulder-in, then travers, then trot on, then travers, then halt, then trot on six or seven strides, then extension. The work is not for the movements themselves but to build up his reactions, how light he is, how he comes back to me.

'Then I started on the lessons of the Grand Prix, the walk, the canter pirouettes, but more on the pick up before the pirouette than the pirouette itself. Then the tempi changes and towards the close of the routine, the piaffe-passage transitions, but very little piaffe because I know the horse well enough and he will not shut off in the arena. I keep him as fresh as I can.

'The only thing that can surprise me in the routine is if the weather changes. At Goodwood it got hot so I walked him more in between, and cut down the work to thirty minutes.' Another variable to the routine is the footing, and 'the exercise ring at Goodwood was deep. To save the horse I tried to ride on the grass to keep out of the deep going.'

A successful warm-up entails very fine tuning, a great knowledge of your horse and a well-thought-through routine. It is this area of the work that can take the longest to discover how to get your horse at his peak just when he is due in the arena. 'It takes a year to produce a top performance with a new horse, to know how to put the horse in the ring to be his best. You can learn to do the movements with him much quicker.'

Another interesting point that Christilot raised was 'if someone computerised the dressage rides they would find it was in the last third where most mistakes were made, which indicates a loss of concentration and lack of condition.' She meant too the condition of the rider as well as the horse and she herself is a very fit person, working just as hard on herself as her horse to keep her mind alert, her body supple and herself strong and healthy.

She also works on her mind. The dressage test in itself does not contain anything frightening like a huge parallel to jump or a coffin to gallop over. Yet riders rarely produce the same form they show at home, because they lose their concentration, relaxation and focus. This might happen because of a fear of the consequences of not doing a movement well, of making a fool of themselves by riding a bad test, of blowing it after having put so much effort, money and time into getting the horse into a position to ride down the centre line at that show.

'Good athletes start to monitor themselves from the time they reach the show site.

Maybe they do not sleep so well. I talk to myself and give a list of reasons why I do not need to worry. I can remembering schooling in the morning at Goodwood and then going off in my hired car. I was getting wound up, and wanted to sort myself out away from the competition. Experience teaches you to monitor yourself, to go away and relax and then come back and start the routine to get ready for the test. Routine is a wonderful thing for the nerves, putting on the bridle and saddle, then that forty-minute warm-up.'

Christilot was made aware of the value of sports psychology at the Montreal Olympics in 1976. 'The story of the Bromont Olympics was an interesting one in my life cycle. There was a lot of pressure, a big build-up for us. The focus was on the Canadian competitors and as I had the best possibilities for Canada there was even more focus on me. My horse pulled a check ligament and right up to the Olympic test I could only walk him and do a few steps of piaffe. My nerves were getting frayed. Georg Theodorescu, our coach, said I could not tell anybody. I was in a tizzy and it was sports psychology time. They gave me a basic course in visualisation and relaxation. I had felt my whole country's hopes were riding on my back, but they got that into focus.' The psychologist asked Christilot to describe the consequences of the test going wrong, to explain how she would react and what she would do. When they actually worked through them, she realised she would not try to commit suicide, she would get up just the same the next morning and go on riding her horse. This made her realise that the consequences were not nearly so bad as she had thought before she had formalised them, and they did not warrant all those nerves generated by that fateful statement, 'What if I blow it?'

The sports psychologist went on to teach her visualisation techniques and that 'was important, because although the horse had been through the trials, and had been high above the others, because of the check ligament I had never ridden the horse outdoors. I visualised a test that flowed and the concentration so high that it felt like it was in slow motion. In a poor performance the rider is late with the aids and always rushing to catch up. It is crucial that the impression of the test is of flow and ease. In visualisation you go through your perfect test.'

With this extraordinary preparation – no cantering or trotting, no real dressage, but plenty of work on the mind – it was even more remarkable that the test went so well and that they finished sixth in the Grand Prix. 'The test did flow, that performance was high above any other I had done. Nobody knew the difficulties behind that ride.'

The sports psychology training had been crucial. 'I had already been doing some of the things they taught me, but it was to what degree you could take it and the consistency you could reach that was important. The worst thing is to hit that ring feeling unprepared.'

Christilot has also had the fortune to work with top-class dressage trainers. It started with Willi Schultheiss, the German national coach, who helped her for the first eight years of her dressage career, but Colonel Handler, the Director the Spanish Riding School, was also a major influence. When on a visit to Canada, she asked him for a textbook used by the Spanish Riding School as she wanted one to help the Canadian

Willi Schultheiss, the great trainer who has been named by so many of the champions as one of their major influences. Here he rides his pupil Cindy Ishoy's Dynasty, showing the exuberant energy described by Christilot Boylen.

riders. He did give her the name of their one textbook and that was de la Guerinière's great book from the eighteenth century. He added the words she has never forgotten: 'Dressage is a verbal tradition', one that is handed down from one generation of riders from the Spanish School to the next; it is not something that is explained easily and precisely in words.

Time with Schultheiss taught her that elusive ability to get the horse 'through' and in front of the leg. 'He rode them so they had great exuberant energy but were often too heavy in the hand for me. It was a time when they wanted those wild extensions. He was a master of positive tension. The horses were power ridden, which looked good but did not feel as relaxed as horses go today. He taught me how to ride a horse that you have to push and those you only have to balance.' He was a master with the Thoroughbreds, the horses that did not need that pushing. The method of training employed by Schultheiss and others in the 1960s and 1970s is one that is getting rarer. The trainer used to ride the horse up to the last possible minute with the pupil sometimes not getting on until just about to enter the arena.

For the next eight years her master was Georg Theodorescu: 'He had a different technique although the classical basis was the same. The horses were different to ride. They were easier to ride; softer and lighter.

'I took the best from both those systems, and any top rider who gets on one of my horses knows it is a Boylen horse. I put great emphasis on being in front of the leg. My forte is to make a horse light and sensitive, and if coupled with the right horse this is a winning factor.

'I am a real stickler for straightness: the balance should be even on both sides. The other major thing is that the horse is sensitive but not frightened. I produce a lady's horse. Male trainers often produce a stronger ratio of hand to leg than I like personally. But a woman can make the adjustments. The same horse can go in a much softer way. '

Today she has special help as she has moved from Canada to live in southern Germany with leading German trainer Udo Lange. He has been Professional Champion of Germany many times and is a product of the German system which is 'big on working the horses over the back, getting them through. The quality of the basic gaits depends on how the horse works over the back. Our relationship is a perfect set-up. There is feedback between the two of us. I have a trained eye always available to help me in my dressage. Also, Udo rides with a two-hole difference in stirrup length. The position we both use is similar. Switching horses between us is not a problem.'

Christilot feels that her Pony Club upbringing in Canada has given her a much greater knowledge of stable management than is normally found in Germany: 'I do the feed programme and it is a happy marriage of the best of both systems. The German dressage system is so strong. There is reason to have very good horses as you can win 90,000DM in a season, and that is an incentive. They have an infrastructure that is lacking in Canada. I felt I was living in a vacuum in

Christilot Boylen, who claimed her Goodwood victory twenty-nine years after she first represented Canada at the Olympics, when she was only seventeen.

Canada, like a sponge wrung out. When you are at the top there is no one to go to, and when you are not going forward, you are going backward.'

With rides in seven Olympics and three decades in top-level dressage, Christilot has a good picture of how the sport has developed. When she started she said about the horses' way of going, 'The necks were much more upright and tight. The highest point was between the ears but they were much shorter in the neck. Today's horses work in a much more balanced frame. They are not so tight in front. The extended trots might not be so brilliant; there is more emphasis now on regularity.'

The area in which dressage has improved dramatically is the piaffe and passage. 'This has much to do with the horses. They are breeding horses in Holland and Germany using certain lines so they are more balanced and have better activity and energy levels for the piaffe and passage. In the past, horses that were brilliant in the piaffe and passage were the exceptions, now many horses are brilliant in these, but there are problems elsewhere. This is also due to the tests as there is more emphasis on the piaffe and passage with more marks being given for these. A horse that it is not good at them you can forget for international dressage.' Certainly the last champion of Goodwood, Biraldo, was.

DOMINIQUE D'ESMÉ

❧❧❧

DOMINIQUE D'ESMÉ won Goodwood in 1975 at the start of her international career as a dressage rider, a career which has taken her to four Olympics, and made her a forerunner in the freestyle to music. Her rhythmic, light and adventurous style of riding is ideal for this medium, and at Goodwood she won two of the freestyles to music on Carioca in 1981, and at Intermédiaire level on Hava in 1983.

She has been one of Goodwood's greatest supporters and most frequent visitors, having competed there on fourteen occasions. 'It was a marvellous event. There was a wonderful ambience. I liked the landscape and the way of life of the English. The English people are indeed the best public in the world, especially for the Kür. We appreciated the quality of the receptions given by the Richmond family in Goodwood House, and the fair play and competence of English competitors like Diana Mason, Jennie Loriston-Clarke and the young Laura Fry.'

Like so many of the top riders Dominique d'Esmé started her dressage career when she was very young, and hers was an even more remarkable start as she was just nine years old when she won her first FEI level test – a Prix St Georges. Her mother, also a dressage rider, has been her daughter's major supporter, along with Christian Gerbaud who goes to all the shows, but Dominique d'Esmé has never had a trainer as such. 'Nobody has trained me. I watch a lot. I used to look at all the riders in competitions. I observed but I worked alone from the start and still do today.'

Dominique d'Esmé takes great pride in her self-made style and is unique amongst the top competitors in never having relied on a trainer. She has always been a very independent personality and after that early start in dressage she left the sport because she disagreed with the judges. She turned to show jumping and three-day eventing and competed at the top national levels in these sports before reverting to dressage when she found Reims. This mare was an outstanding athlete by Brule Tout and out of a Vol de Nuit mare. They soon earned a place on the French team, which was fourth in the 1974 World Championships. In that year too they came to the first Goodwood CDI and won the first of their fourteen National Dressage Championships.

At those Goodwood Championships in 1975 the crowd were delighted by their style

Thor, who took Dominique d'Esmé to her third World Cup Final in 1991.

Dominique d'Esmé won her first Prix St Georges at nine years of age. She has brought France much glory in freestyle to music.

of dressage. Their very round, light, forward work was more understandable to the layman in the British Isles than the more disciplined style of many of the winners. It was not an easy win as they had to perform their test in one of those freak storms that hit Goodwood. The hail was so thick, that when Dominique d'Esmé bowed her head in the salute, the ice slid off the edge of her hat and 'there was enough for ten glasses of whisky!'

Reims took Dominique to her first Olympics in Montreal in 1976, and Dominique is proud of the fact that the mare remained in her stables until she died at the great age of thirty-two.

Dominique has trained an impressive number of horses to be good enough to win Grands Prix and take her into French teams. Carioca, Fresh Wind, Hopal Fleury, Thor, Rapport and Arnoldo Thor have all been successful international Grand Prix horses with her. At first she used French-bred horses, but it was difficult to find them with the talent for dressage. In France the emphasis has been on the show jumper. Breeders and riders focus on this sport, and with considerable success, but at the expense of producing the dressage horse. Riders have been forced to buy abroad and both Thor and Rapport were Westphalians, and Arnoldo Thor, Dutch. Thor is a stallion and has been chosen by a French selection committee as a sire that could help to produce French-born dressage horses. The scheme is called Plus de Dressage and Dominique d'Esmé is a member of the panel that selects the stallions and mares. She says, 'The French dressage horse is evolving.'

At her home at Pont-l'Evêque in Normandy she does not breed horses but she has fifteen dressage horses in work and finds time between shows to teach other riders.

Dominique d'Esmé is playing her part to encourage France to breed as good dressage horses as she does show jumpers, but Dominique's special skill and great love is the creation of the musical freestyle. 'I am not a musician, but I do like music.' She explains that it is the tempo and cadence of the horse that is important, and these are never the same for any two horses. Each horse's music is individual to him, and she never uses the same tapes for different horses.

In the choreography she is famous for her daring patterns and original movements. She feels it is important for the movements to be difficult and avoids using the same figures as in the straight tests.

Despite having made numerous freestyle programmes for her horses she says there is

Dominique d'Esmé with Thor, showing off the free, rounded trot that epitomises her style of dressage.

no routine to the work – 'It depends on the horses' – and she relies on 'moments of inspiration'. Again her creations are entirely hers: 'There is no outside influence. The final choice is inside the family and made by my mother, myself and from my video. We sit beside the burning fireplace in winter.'

Two decades of international dressage competitions have not diminished her enthusiasm, nor her capacity to improve. She feels that her Kür at the 1994 World Cup Finals was her best to date, and there was no doubt of her enjoyment at winning the Kür at the Addington CDI of 1994, twenty years after she made her first appearance in Britain.

Dominique d'Esmé feels the freestyle is the best opportunity the sport of dressage has to progress. It is what the people come to watch. 'It has been the best development in dressage.'

CINDY ISHOY

❧·❧·❧

CINDY ISHOY (formerly Neale) set a string of records when she won the 1979 Goodwood Championship. She became the first Canadian to win an international dressage competition in Europe. She completed a quadruple, taking the Grand Prix and Kür with Martyr and the Prix St Georges and Intermédiaire with Equus. But most notable of all, she was the first rider to win an international Kür to music as this was the inaugural competition under FEI rules, and a historic one as it was to change the nature of competitive dressage.

The most stunning part of her Kür had been the pirouettes, which she rode as double ones, and although today they are a regular feature in Kürs, in those days they were not a requirement in Grand Prix and few had ever seen them. The most surprising aspect of the test, considering how today's Kürs are so professionally choreographed, was the lack of preparation. As she explained to journalists afterwards: 'I had no preconceived ideas. I simply rode the movements as I felt Martyr was ready for them.'

These wins had a huge impact on Cindy and on Canada's dressage: 'They gave me the inspiration to carry on with an international competitive career. They made the Canadians accept me as an international competitor and made international judges aware of Canadian riders. This paved the way for future Canadian competitors.'

Cindy proved that these successes were no fluke, going on to win at Fontainebleau that same year. Nor did

Cindy Ishoy on her most talented horse, Dynasty, with whom she won her greatest honour, a team bronze at the 1988 Olympics. They were the best of the Canadians, taking fourth place individually.

they come out of the blue, for the previous year she had been fifth in Aachen and had taken part in the 1978 World Championships where she achieved the highest-ever place for a Canadian, finishing eighth individually. When she came out of the arena from riding the Grand Prix Special test 'I remember my trainer, Schultheiss, stood up and clapped and told me that it was the most aggressively ridden test of the day. During the ceremony I stood amongst all those great riders in a state of disbelief; it went by as if I was on the outside looking in – it was a dream.'

It was not, however, all joy at Goodwood and there were challenges other than just riding the tests. 'My trainer's wife had an accident because she drove on the wrong side of the road. I, also, always started off from the stables driving on the 'wrong' side, but by the time I got to the end of the road in the park I had usually realised, although once almost too late when we nearly ran into the American team!'

Cindy had one great advantage over other Canadian riders, namely that her father had been stationed in Germany with the Royal Canadian Air Force. It mean she started dressage when she was just thirteen years of age and had some correct tuition even if it was only at the local riding school of Zweibrucken. At nineteen she was in the Canadian team that went to the Pan-Am Games where they won the team gold medal and she was fourth individually. Then at just twenty years old she went to the 1972 Munich Olympics on Bonne Année.

Her first international winner, Martyr, was bought in Germany in 1974 and, although already trained, she says, 'he was a very inexpensive horse. He was a very difficult horse to ride. I did not ride him before I bought him. I just watched Schultheiss ride him and then had him shipped to Canada. When he arrived and I started riding him I realised he was very difficult. When he made his mind up about something it was very difficult to change it. He went over backwards several times. He taught me to be very humble and that dressage is a give-and-take relationship between horse and rider. We came to an understanding. In the warm-ups we rarely practised anything in the test and he put out maximum in the ring. With Martyr you always asked, you never told him.'

Cindy was a talented rider but without the funds needed to realise it; moreover she lived in a country that was starved of top trainers and competitions essential to develop ability. Her great fortune was her friendship with Dinny Day, who died in 1983. 'She believed in me and supported me morally when no one else believed in me. She encouraged me through the tough times.' It was Dinny Day's parents, Mr and Mrs Burns who bought Cindy Martyr, Equus, her greatest star Dynasty, and her latest prospect Donevan. They are lucky owners – in another sphere, their steeplechaser Highland Wedding won the Grand National. 'Without the Burns I would not have had an international career.'

They helped her too with the other great expense of becoming a dressage star in Canada: 'the cost of travel to Europe to compete and train.' For five years (1975 – 1980) Cindy spent most of her time in Germany, at the national centre at Warendorf, working with the great Willi Schultheiss and Siegfried Peilicke. 'They moulded my riding style and made me the rider that I am today.'

'I want my horses to go obediently, but without overpowering their grace, and for their natural gaits and beauty to be enhanced. The rider must be complementary to the horse and not distract from the horse's gymnastic strength to allow them to perform with the beauty and grace of a dancer.'

This approach towards her riding made her a 'natural' for the more artistic form of dressage, the music freestyles, and ever since that inaugural victory at Goodwood she has been a great supporter of these classes. 'Freestyle is getting a lot more emphasis. This is very positive, particularly in that it is a selling point for the sport in Canada.'

With Dynasty she put on some great performances in the early years of the World Cup, qualifying twice for the final. In 1987 she was an unlucky fourth (one judge placed her first in the freestyle) and the following year almost came out on top, but Christine Stückelberger managed to retain the title with Gaugin de Lully. Dynasty was, however, gaining more and more admirers, and at the Olympics he was the major contributor towards the Canadian's bronze team medal and he himself only just missed an individual one, coming fourth. Tragically, his promising career was brought to an end by colic and his early death.

Martyr and Cindy Ishoy, the Goodwood Champions of 1979. Martyr was a very difficult horse who taught his rider humility, and that dressage is a give-and-take relationship.

A wonderfully expressive flying change from Equus, the horse who won the Prix St Georges and Intermédiaire at Goodwood in 1979, for his rider Cindy Ishoy.

Cindy served her apprenticeship in Germany but she has remained a great promoter of Canada. 'My most important goal is to train my own horse in Canada to Grand Prix and to encourage and build up dressage in Canada. I would also like to represent Canada with quality tests and horses.' Her major assistant now is her husband Neil, who manages Ishoy Enterprise Stables in Ontario. 'My husband and I work together and we have sent several successful young riders to the North American Championships.'

She is giving assistance and inspiration to her compatriots but it was at Goodwood that she got so much of hers: 'The very enthusiastic crowd was always a plus for riders and competitors. They were inspiring and exciting. Goodwood has a beautiful setting with areas to graze your horse and hack. The stabling facilities were wonderful. From a Canadian point of view it was a wonderful experience to go through Goodwood House as British history is very much a part of Canadian history.'

REINER KLIMKE

❧❧❧

THE GREATEST OF the Goodwood Champions must be Dr Reiner Klimke. He has done so much more than win dressage competitions. A full-time lawyer, he has trained more horses to Grand Prix in his spare time than any other competitor even when devoting their lives to it. He has won an incredible seven Olympic gold medals, been the individual European Champion on three different horses, and the World Champion on two different ones. He has won more FEI Championships than anyone else and was just nineteen years of age when, at his first European Championships (1955), he won the Prix St Georges. He has also put so much back into his sport, not only as an administrator but also through devising, lecturing and writing about a system of training which is easy to follow and which has helped riders of the calibre of Ferdi Eilberg, Jo Hinnemann and his two children, Ingrid and Michael, to become top international competitors.

He was a regular visitor to Goodwood, starting with a trip in 1977 when as the reigning World Champion he came to reconnoitre the grounds for the following year when he would defend his title. He brought Mehmed, and impressed all with his single-mindedness. The British were amazed to see the World Champion crossing his stirrups and riding without them in the riding-in. And then there was his obvious high level of extraordinary concentration, both in the riding-in and in the test. He duly won the Championship but sadly for him it was the last with Mehmed. The horse was sixteen years and 'becoming older, but then he had a nice life, eleven more years in my stable'. He became a very special schoolmaster, living in an equally special stable, which Dux (European Champion, Olympic individual bronze and twice team gold medallist) had used in his retirement and Ahlerich (European, World and Olympic Champion) occupied in his retirement years from 1988 to 1992.

That first trip to Goodwood had its problems and, as for so many riders, they were encountered on the journey. 'I had heard so much about Goodwood. We were very interested and a little bit nervous about what would be there. But we could not find it. We had problems driving on the left and there were no signs to Goodwood. It took us one or two hours to find it.'

Once there, Reiner and Ruth Klimke were impressed. They appreciated the friendly atmosphere and particularly enjoyed dining at Goodwood House, because 'we could see part of your culture'. Another feature they liked was the changelessness of Goodwood. When they came back for the sixth time in 1991 'we still saw the same people'.

In 1978, instead of defending his title, he was there as a television commentator. 'It was a good Championship. Granat and Slibowitz were very close, but it was not so strong as in 1966 or 1974 because unfortunately on that day Granat had too many mistakes and Slibowitz had wonderful movements but he could not do piaffe. The atmosphere was fantastic. It was real international sport.'

His comments about Jennie Loriston-Clarke and Dutch Courage helped draw attention to her. 'She had no name then. I said from a technical point of view they were the best because there were no mistakes, and good piaffe and passage changes. It was the best performance I saw from her. I remember I said she will win a medal.'

Other comments he made at that Championship were soon circulating. 'People thought I was finished because I had retired Mehmed, but I had just started with Ahlerich and at Aachen he had won the Little Tour. When people asked what I was

Dr Reiner Klimke rides his World and Goodwood Champion Mehmed in a bold canter.

Reiner Klimke shows that even the great riders keep using the basic methods of learning; here he rides without stirrups prior to competing at the 1980 Alternative Olympics.

doing I would reply that I had the next World Champion in my stable. I was joking, but it turned out to be true.'

Dr Klimke brought Ahlerich, the best horse he ever had, to Goodwood twice. The first time was their debut on the German team for the Alternative Olympics in 1980, and the next was in 1981 when, for the second time, he became a Goodwood Champion.

'I had difficult times at Goodwood with my friend Ahlerich. Twice he was bad in the Grand Prix and then mild in the Special. You could see very far and the television cameras were high behind the judges' boxes. He was more interested in those than in me. In the two Grands Prix, in the extended trots, he jumped into canter. He was like a young horse, but on the Special days he was good. In 1980 he had a very good Special.' They earned their first individual medal for this, the bronze.

The reason for his trip in 1981 shows the depth of thinking that went behind making Ahlerich a European, World and Olympic Champion. His goal was the 1982 World

Championships. Granat was coming to the end of his career but the World Championships were in his home country. Christine Stückelberger would have the assets of sentimentality and a home crowd on her side; Dr Klimke and Ahlerich would find it hard to beat them, but the lawyer was a skilled tactician as well as a great rider.

Gustav Nyblaeus was the going to be the President of the Jury at the World Championships and he always came to Goodwood to judge. Dr Klimke recalls his strategy: 'I always followed Nyblaeus with Ahlerich. If I wanted to become World Champion, then I had to convince Nyblaeus, and in the first years he did not like him. I could not escape from this so I went wherever he was judging. He was a strong person, sometimes very severe. He was a fanatic about correct rhythm, and in principle I could understand this, but you can have a horse with a fantastic trot and there is a hole and he makes an uneven step and is down to a three, and then a horse with no trot and the judges give a four because he is regular.' This the doctor found hard to accept, especially as he was a frequent victim. With Ahlerich's brilliance and freedom in his paces any slight unlevelness was much more obvious than for a horse with a restricted trot.

The finest hour for Dr Reiner Klimke and Ahlerich at the 1984 Olympics where they performed their most memorable tests to win the team and individual gold.

Dr Reiner Klimke shows the concentration that has been a key factor in his success.

'Ahlerich could easily become tense behind because he was oversensitive. His father was a racehorse. When he was tense he hopped behind, and to relax him needed one and a half hours' work. I agreed with Nyblaeus; I did not like this, but it was difficult to change him!'

Nor did Nyblaeus waver in what he believed was right. 'I admired him because he really judged what he saw. Nobody could influence him. He was absolutely straight. But he did not mind so much about the neck. The horses could be short in the neck and he could still give high marks.'

Nyblaeus was eventually convinced about Ahlerich and he did win that 1982 World Championship, although his best test of all was two years later at the Olympics. 'He did a super Grand Prix in Los Angeles.' The doctor added, 'I lost many competitions but knew when he went well nobody could beat him.' In all, he won one hundred Grands Prix during his great career, including that 1981 Goodwood Grand Prix Special.

Ahlerich was a 'super' horse, and he had appeared to be so when he was bought for Dr Klimke as the top-priced horse at the 1975 Westphalian auctions, costing DM42,000. But even super horses have problems: apart from that high-spirited temperament coming from his Thoroughbred father, Angelo, there were deficits in conformation that lesser riders might not have overcome. 'When Ahlerich was young he was a weak horse, sensitive in his back. It took time for him to get enough muscles to carry the rider without tension. You can fix problems if you have enough patience and do enough work. We did a lot of outside work, going up and down hills, cavellettis, trot/walk transitions and we made it OK. But then he became so strong he needed so much work to settle him!'

Dr Klimke is, however, a maestro at getting horses to use their backs and to work through them. This comes from his system of training and from the way he rides. 'When I am riding I very seldom sit strong or sit behind the vertical. My influence should come from the legs and not so much from the back. When I want to push, I use the legs. With my seat I try to go with the horse.' He eagerly proved this point, that is contrary to traditional ideas of strong-disciplined German riding, by showing a picture of his brilliant Russian stallion Biotop in an extended trot and with him sitting not even upright but just slightly in front of the vertical.

Perhaps the most far-reaching development in modern dressage is the increasing emphasis put on the use of the horse's back, and the horse's ability to use it so that the paces become more elastic and more brilliant. The doctor talked about Willi Schultheiss, the trainer whose work had been so influential through the 1960s and 1970s. 'His horses worked very high in front but not so much behind and were not so good in the back. We have improved. More horses work from behind over the back to the hands. But now some riders overdo it. They say they push from behind but then they pull from in front. The horse's back rounds up so much that it gets a high point and if the rider sits heavily it gets sore. You should leave the back in a more natural position with the horses working long and low and taking the hands. That is enough. The best measure of how well a horse steps under is when the rider gives the reins and the horse stretches his neck. It only happens if you have a contact and ride from behind over the back and into the mouth.'

The doctor is wary of the extreme ways of suppling the horse that are practised by so many of the riders today. His theories are simple and have not changed since he wrote about them in his book *Basic Training of the Young Horse*, published in 1984. 'The theory is very simple, but the practice is more difficult because horses have nerves and temperaments.

'But we must keep the system simple and must believe that it is easy to do. If we think it is difficult, it will become difficult. When we teach we must say it is very simple then they can do it.' A little bit of positive-thinking and sports psychology have crept into the system.

Those who want to learn about the way Klimke trains can watch the riders at the St Georg Hall on the outskirts of Münster. His horses have been kept there since he took to serious dressage. One of the only major differences today is that it has become a 'United Nations' of the horse world. On the day I was there, riders came from the USA and Russia as well as from Germany, and onlookers even included visitors from India. There is almost a reverential air, with one American student saying it was like working with a Michelangelo. The hours with the maestro are, however, extremely limited as he can only escape from his work to be with the horses during the lunch hour and at weekends.

The system, however, is so well established that it is easier for the riders to be confident of the way of working. The formula is consistent: first the loosening work, then the work period and finally the cooling-off. 'We train the horse in three parts. First the loosening-up, long and low but still with the nose in front of the vertical. For moments the nose can come behind – this is OK, and sometimes we play a little with the reins to make them supple. Then we give them a little break, and you must have ideas as to what you intend to do in the work section. You need a little programme of work to make the horses better. Each horse has his problems and you must find how to solve them, but by explaining not forcing. Both rider and horse must enjoy the work. This is the essence of success.'

In the work section the rider has to plan how to combine the principles that are the

Dr Reiner Klimke and Ahlerich survey the scene at Goodwood. Ahlerich's intelligent, alert outlook is very-obvious.

Gustav Nyblaeus, who as Chairman of the FEI Dressage Committee guided dressage through the 1970s and early 1980s, and as a judge took time to be convinced that Ahlerich deserved the top marks.

base of all real German training: *losgelassenheit*, *takt*, contact, *schwung*, straightness and collection. Developing these training scales, as they are known, is the way to develop the horse's natural ability. The final stage is for cooling off and relaxing, when again the horses are allowed to stretch forward and down and walk on a free rein. This is a reward but also a test, because they will only want to take the rein gently if they have been working correctly over their backs.

Dr Klimke is old enough to have worked with great names like Gustav Rau, and later Paul and Albert Stecken, who helped him formulate his views. 'I was very lucky because I had the opportunity to ride with the best people,' he says. But then came the unusual factor – his first Olympic sport was the three-day event and he rode for Germany in the Rome Olympics: 'I was influenced by my three-day event riding because then you really feel the horse. You feel his nature. You must trust each other and learn to feel what is in the horse. It is difficult for riders who have only done dressage to feel what is condition. You cannot present the movements well when a horse is not in condition and you cannot bring out condition in a horse by making him tired.'

Horsemanship is a key element in becoming a really good rider and the doctor's daughter, Ingrid, is following in his footsteps. She is an international event rider and at a recent Westphalian Auction Gala evening she rode her horse Patriot over very high fences, then changed into a tail coat and rode through the Grand Prix movements. She, like her father, has learnt to feel what is in the horse.

The Klimkes put great emphasis on what is natural for the horse, on developing pride, presence and the muscles that give him that air of nobility. 'It is very important that the neck is built up from the withers. You need to build up the muscles along the topline in the neck and you can only do this if you push into quiet hands. If the horse goes along for himself then you do not need to push. The feel in both hands should be equal and it comes from behind, it comes from my legs.'

Klimke is very happy that increasing numbers of riders are treating the horse more like a person and less like an object. 'The rider must build up his personality. People come to shows to watch Biotop competing, not because of technical things but because he is happy and proud.'

'Our aim in our gymnastic training must be that the horse becomes more beautiful and healthy. If he becomes uneven and stiff he will not be more healthy.'

Over the years that Dr Klimke has been competing (forty years at international level), he is happy that there have been two particularly important improvements with young people being successful and the higher quality of horses. 'Especially in Germany, dressage has become a sport for the young people. We used to think you had to be fifty years old to become a perfect rider, as was the case with Lorke and Schultheiss. Then Nicole won the Olympics at twenty-two. It has been a good development to open the sport to young people who want to ride dressage. In Germany we invest a lot of money in young riders. We do more for the young than for their elders.'

The other important improvement is: 'We have better horses. In Germany and Holland we produce better horses. I look back to Mehmed. This horse would not have been good enough today. We now have more elegant horses that do not need strength to ride.'

This makes possible probably the most important development of all and that is the type of partnership between the horse and his rider. 'It came from the cavalry that you needed one hundred per cent obedience from your horse, but my horse is not my slave. He is my friend. This must be in the head of today's riders and then they can build up a good combination.'

It is important for riders and trainers to keep abreast of current thinking in international dressage, and to be made aware of developments – like that dressage riding is not domination, that international judges want to see regular, supple horses, and that the lighter, more elegant horses are becoming more successful than the powerful heavy ones. This is all learnt by watching top international riders. 'Without Goodwood you would not have dressage in England. International events are the way to learn. Goodwood brought dressage to the UK. Everybody who had eyes could see the international standards and what you had to work for to reach them. This is the influence and the luck that you had Goodwood.'

Dr Klimke now has a horse with even more charisma than Ahlerich. His Russian stallion Biotop has that air of greatness in his expression that reminds one of Milton and Desert Orchid. He says he is training him for his son Michael to take over, and adds poignantly: 'It would have been a good end to my career to ride Biotop at Goodwood.'

PIA LAUS

꧁ ꧂

PIA LAUS was the youngest ever Goodwood Champion, winning the Grand Prix and Special in 1991 when she was twenty-three years old. This was her first major win in senior international dressage, which is surprising considering her remarkable record of getting into every single ride-off for the individual title whether it was European, World or Olympics, for eight successive years, from 1986 to 1993. Admittedly, the first four were at Young Rider level, when she won four team gold medals, two individual golds and one individual silver.

She and her little Westphalian stallion, Adrett, by Adlerfels, won the hearts of the British people. Pia explains: 'It was the first time people recognised I had a special relationship with my horse. The British have a feeling for horsemanship, and they came up to me to say they could see it.

'Our horses are part of our family.' Almost literally, for at her home on the side of a hill overlooking the heart of Germany's industrial lands in Westphalia, there is just enough room to squeeze in the stables that house her nine horses and a goat, with a minute paddock dividing them from the house.

Her first pony is still in residence and 'comes inside the house to take breakfast with me! I so like to have the horses near me.'

The Laus family became steeped in the horse world and this despite nobody in the family having been in the remotest bit horsey. The genes were there, however, as a great grandfather had ridden at Potsdam. Pia, as a child, kept on wanting to be with horses and when she was eight years old it all started when she was given her first pony – the one that breakfasts with her. The dressage began, as it does in Germany, with regional competitions and success in these whetted the appetite, so much so that Pia's mother decided a horse was needed. Not knowing any better she selected a three-year-old stallion for her thirteen-year-old daughter. Mrs Laus says: 'All the teachers told me to buy an older horse, but I said we would buy him.' To cement the audacity of doing such a crazy thing, albeit in ignorance, she bought the four-year-old Liebenberg as a Christmas present for Pia.

Today those two purchases, that nobody with any knowledge of horses would have

One of the spectacular extensions that helped Adrett and Pia Laus to win at Goodwood.

Pia Laus and Adrett on their way into the Goodwood arena where they had so much success.

ever made for a teenager without any background in horses, are Pia's international partners that have taken her all over the world, including to the Olympics. Pia admits, 'It was luck; it was not clever, only luck.'

Her mother did, however, ensure that as soon as her daughter showed her talent she had top-class assistance. At fourteen she was successful in the Westphalian Championships and Heinz Lammers, winner at Goodwood in 1974, took over as trainer. When successful at national level, the national coach Harry Boldt was asked to give her instruction and with four Young Rider team golds and three individual medals hanging on her walls, she moved on to maestro Dr Schulten-Baumer. 'I think sometimes you have to change. You need new ideas. When you are young you have to learn from everybody.'

For three years she took in his unique system and for the last four has worked on her own. Her mother, who only sat on a horse once and got off after one round, is now her assistant. 'My mother always had to drive me and was always watching.' Her mother adds, 'My hobby is Pia and the horses, and from watching every day you can learn so much.'

Pia, despite having the intellect to qualify as a lawyer, does not rely on dressage books. The only one she has read seriously is that of Plinzner which Stecken, one of Germany's greatest dressage experts, told her to read.

'I am still riding Schulten-Baumer's way, but it would have been difficult to start with his method. First you have to learn the basics of riding thoroughly, then you can find other ways. To start in dressage you have to learn how to sit on the horse and to work with the horse in the classical way. I would not want to start the Schulten-Baumer way without understanding how the horses have to go.'

Those early trainers followed the basic German system – as Harry Boldt put it, the golden thread of rhythm, suppleness, contact, impulsion and collection. Only when a rider can train these into a horse is she ready to develop the more extreme ways of suppling the horse.

Pia places enormous emphasis on the character of the horse. 'It is most important that the horse likes to work and be friends with me.' A ten-minute walk through the woods to the riding school where she works helps give them a refreshing start and finish to their work. But she also works them in the woods, and when the fields are cut they get a canter on the grass.

The key to her success is the relationship between horse and rider: 'Adrett loves me and I love him. In the test he is always fighting on my side. We are a great team. His strong point is his extended trot – it feels like flying.'

She has a strong team of horses coming up behind her current international partners, although they have done little competing. She has a ten-year-old, a seven-year-old and two five-year-olds. All were chosen with much more thought than her two current partners. The five-year-old Exquisite, by Ecuador, was bought from a farmer when only two, but only after two trips to Hanover to look at him and one trip to Poland to see if there was anything better. Pia admitted afterwards: 'At first sight I fell in love with him,' but she did not tell anybody until they were all sure he was the right one.

Pia's problem is finding the time to compete them. Apart from the lengthy trips to international shows with her top pair, there are those law exams, and, when qualified, a career as a lawyer to pursue. She feels she rides better when she has other things to do. Once she concentrated solely on the horses for six months and found she became too intense, placing too much emphasis on whether a horse went badly or well.

She has nevertheless found time to fit in being team trainer to the Italian Young

Pia Laus takes pride in establishing a close relationship with her horses and helps to look after them.

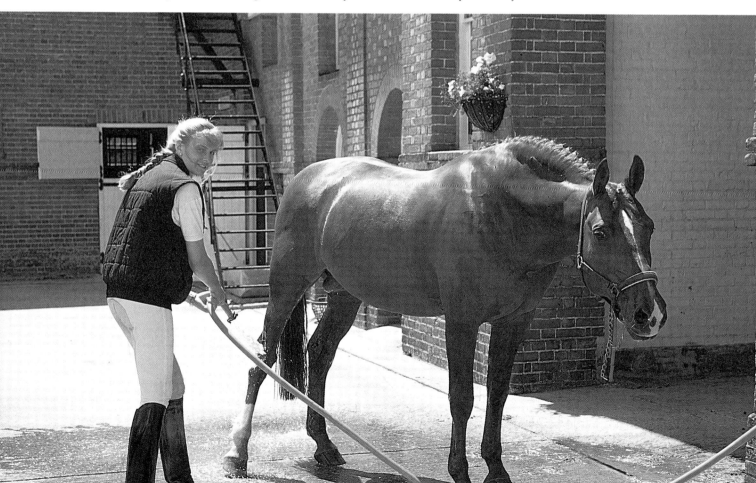

The wonderfully crested neck of the stallion Adrett.

Riders. Having the option to take an Italian passport because of her late father's nationality, she did so when she graduated from Young Riders. She trained the Italian youngsters for the 1993 Championship at Spangenberg, but there were problems. 'In Italy they do not learn to grow up with ponies. The young riders have good horses but they should learn to live with them. They need to understand their horses, to know how they are eating and feeling every day. Now when I go to a show I can see how Adrett is, when he is not in a good mood and when I have to give him carrots to make him better. They do not understand this.'

With the value she places on developing sensitivity towards the feelings of her horses, it is not surprising that she enjoyed England and Goodwood. 'Goodwood was the nicest of all the outdoor shows,' and this despite it being 'the most horrible drive – we were in a big jam for three hours on the M20 and we said we would never come again. Then when we got there everything was so nice and the people were so friendly.

'I came without thinking of winning. I always try to do my best, but just before, in Aachen, they [the horses] were not running very well, but at Goodwood they were going forward again. When I beat Isabell [Werth], by one point, Dr Schulten-Baumer was angry because it was only one point, but I said to him, "One point is one point!"'

JENNIE LORISTON-CLARKE

J ENNIE LORISTON-CLARKE and Goodwood go together like a horse and carriage. She is the only rider to have competed and won prizes at every single Goodwood International. Most of the highlights in her illustrious competitive career were at Goodwood, and many of these moments have been landmarks in Britain's own development as a dressage nation.

It was Jennie Loriston-Clarke who was the first to have the national anthem played for her, signalling a home victory for a British rider (Goodwood 1980); it was Jennie Loriston-Clarke who was the first British person to win at a European Championships,

A family affair – two sons of Dutch Courage who have competed successfully internationally, Catherston Dazzler (left), ridden by Jennie Loriston-Clarke, and Catherston Dutch Bid, ridden by Jennie's daughter Lizzie.

albeit a Prix St Georges (Goodwood 1987); it was Jennie Loriston-Clarke who was the first British rider to win a Freestyle at a championship (Goodwood 1987); and it was Jennie Loriston-Clarke who was the only British rider in the Grand Prix at the first CDI (Goodwood 1974). But most memorably and most influential of all, it was Jennie Loriston-Clarke who won the individual bronze medal at the 1978 World Championships, and it was this success that gave Britain the boost she needed gradually to turn into a nation which valued, appreciated and was good at dressage. More emotionally and sentimentally it was at Goodwood that the then Countess of March held a tea party and final parade in honour of Jennie's partner in most of these successes, Dutch Courage.

Jennie Loriston-Clarke has been a pillar around which British dressage has developed. Her horsemanship, successes, enthusiasm and eagerness to let others share her knowledge and experience, have been instrumental in giving the inspiration needed for dressage to progress.

Jennie's riding career began in the show ring. As one of the six children in the famous Bullen family, she practised all manner of equestrian activities but the focus in the early years was on showing, with ponies bred mostly by her parents. The basis of her equestrian education included winning championships at the Royal International, the Horse of the Year Show, the Richmond and Royal Windsor shows, and taking leading roles in displays put on at major events – all of which were highly suitable training for a future dressage champion. It was an education which did not include going to school, though, for with so much to do at home and so many brothers and sisters, a governess was a viable alternative.

Although Jennie evented and show jumped it was as a show rider that she became most famous, but not for long. When she had made Desert Storm Hack of the Year for the third year running, an announcement was made while she rode under the spotlight during her lap of honour. They were retiring to take up dressage. This was the kind of assistance this isolated minority sport needed. In the following quarter century she and Goodwood have been the key factors in its development and have given dressage more assistance than one could have possibly imagined.

Jennie was a naturally gifted horsewoman but her riding was underpinned by her Pony Club upbringing with its traditional British approach towards equitation. Whilst it made great jumping and galloping riders, it was not geared to producing good dressage ones. All of this slowed down her early progress as a dressage rider, but her problem was also Britain's problem and helps to explain the enormous length of time it took Britain, a country of horsemen, to establish itself as a nation of dressage riders.

'When I started in dressage the emphasis was on obedience. I was not taught about suppleness of the back and engagement. It never came into my thinking. We did not understand about it in England, and I don't think it was taught very well by the foreign masters. Perhaps it was a language problem, but the British did not pick it up.'

OPPOSITE: *Dutch Gold, the near-thoroughbred son of Dutch Courage, who like his father excelled at piaffe.*

Jennie explains, 'You have to make the horses very responsive to forward and downward transitions so they can sit and are soft in their backs. It is a principle that I did not appreciate early enough in my life nor how to train to achieve it. I did not know enough to be able to make the horse sufficiently elastic to go forward and back. I did not make the horses elastic enough before going sideways, but started fiddling about with the movements and ruined the paces. Once there is some collection and lightness of the forehand then you can get better shoulder-in and half-passes. When the horses can sit more then you can get those lovely half passes when they barely touch the ground. When they are lighter in the shoulders they can do the lateral work so much better.'

This was probably the key factor in Britain's disappointing progress in dressage. In competitions the foreign judges wanted a horse that showed expression, brilliance of its paces and roundness of outline. In Britain we wanted a horse that was responsive, light and obedient, that was a good ride in the show ring, in the hunting field or into fences. The former needed a rider that was supple, balanced and upright and dared the horse to develop its power; the latter could be ridden through communication with the mind and the reins, which did not develop the horse's athleticism. Through the 1960s and 70s it was the Spanish Riding School that was Britain's 'god', and although much was learnt from its teaching, because the expression of the paces was of secondary importance this was a handicap in the international competition arena. Jennie cited Gunnar Anderson, the great Danish trainer, as one who did emphasise athleticism in his courses, but 'I did not understand. He was too advanced for me at that stage of my training. He was one of the most brilliant trainers. I wish I had known more to have been able to understand him better.'

Jennie talked about another problem that hampered Britain's development: the importance attached to the expression 'sitting deep'. 'It was the wrong expression. It was a translation from the German which got the wrong idea across. It is not sitting deep but raising the diaphragm. If the rider sits upright enough he can balance the horse with his seat.' The misconception about sitting deep led to riders sitting heavily and forcefully making it difficult for their horses to move through the back and develop expression in their paces. So Britain's difficulties in understanding what competitive dressage was about were due in part to language problems. Dressage expressions were misunderstood with the foreign masters saying one thing but the British interpreting it as something else. Translation led to confusion. German, the language of the leading dressage nation, is a very precise tongue and there are no English counterparts for crucial words like *Schwung*, *Takt* and *Kreutz*. Jennie maintains, 'It is difficult to get things expressed correctly so that the rider can give the right feeling to the horse.' She remembers seeing Podhajsky take off his shirt to gallop a horse around an arena and show how he braced his back muscles to get him to collect.

The language barrier did not stop Jennie from being successful. On Desert Storm she represented Britain abroad, and her next international partner, Kadett, took her to the 1972 Munich Olympics. When Goodwood started in 1973 she had found her greatest partner, the Dutch Warmblood stallion Dutch Courage, known to all his friends as 'Bill'.

'Bill had a special personality. It was the way he looked at you. The best horses are the ones that look at you. They treat you with respect, as another being. Others look over you and treat you as a means of getting food. The best look at you as a companion, but only a few of my horses have given me that feeling – the ponies Silver Moon, Bubbly and Anthony Adverse; and the stallions Xenocles, Bill, Dutch Gold and Dazzler. They nicker at me and appreciate me. Kadett and Desert Storm were aloof and did not give me the same feeling and we never had quite that same rapport. When I first saw Bill I knew he was the sort of horse who would look at me and listen to me. That is what makes the best partnership.'

She found Bill in a Dutch dealer's yard. She was drawn to him when she saw him looking out of his stable, and turned down those she was supposed to like in favour of this stallion who was bred to jump, not to do dressage, his sire being the French Thoroughbred Millerole, who produced a number of international show jumpers.

Mrs Steele came into partnership with Jennie, having previously owned Kadett. 'There were moments when I thought I had bitten off more than I could chew. As a three-year-old, when I was riding him in the New Forest that surrounded our Catherston Stud, he was quite hairy to sit on. He could put in a fair buck. But in the forest it was OK because you knew you could go for one and a half miles before having to pull up. He was quite wild to start with and tried to tell the world he was here all the time, but he soon learnt in that first year not to neigh when ridden. All the horses I have got on best with have been characters, and in some way were special personalities. They had playful ways that could take some sitting. The most difficult to sit on is Dazzler – he is so powerful.'

Stars in all sports need strong personalities, but what most people admire in dressage horses are spectacular paces. Yet of all Jennie's international partners few have been flamboyant movers as youngsters. Dutch Courage, Dutch Gold and Catherston Dazzler looked quite ordinary when they moved and there was no sign of the brilliance of movement most seek when trying to buy a top-class horse. 'Bill had a lot of activity but not a lot of swing. He did not have spectacular paces. He was bred to be a show jumper. When I first looked at him I thought he was a cross between Merely a Monarch and Lauriston, and I thought he could go show jumping or eventing if he did not make a dressage horse.

'Dutch Bid was my most spectacular mover but he was the one who found it difficult to collect. He had freedom without activity. The others had the activity and produced the freedom as they got further up the ladder.'

Jennie warns about some of the hazards of looking for spectacular movement: 'Particularly abroad they excite them so much they look like good movers, but it is not natural movement.

'The Germans and Dutch produce some tremendous movers but some can seem extravagant because they put a lot of power into the normal trot, yet they do not have much more for the extended trot. Horses with elevated trots sail through novice but when they have to produce power, elevation and collection they find it more difficult.'

Bill's lack of natural freedom meant that he never earned the higher marks for his extended trot, but this was offset by the fact that his balanced correct paces made the collected movements easier. Added to this was his quick mind that, in the hands of a rider with whom he had established such a rapport, made him a very fast learner. At just nine years of age he gave British dressage its most dramatic day in its entire history.

'I can vividly remember every moment of his bronze medal test,' says Jennie, but the build-up to this extraordinary occasion, which was featured on the national TV news and earned Jennie an MBE, had been pretty hair-raising. With this being the first time that the world's best exponents of this mysterious sport had competed in Britain, there had been some media hype. As the country's leading combination, having been ninth at the previous year's European Championships, Jennie and Bill found themselves on the front page of the *Sunday Telegraph* colour supplement. It put Jennie under pressure: 'It did little for my feeling of security, having my name in the paper. If I did badly it would not have enhanced dressage.'

The worst did happen. Bill blew up in their first test, the Intermédiaire II. 'He was very fresh and I was very nervous; we made many mistakes. I came out desperately disappointed. I had not given him enough work. I knew there was no use in producing him in the Grand Prix unless I trained him in the way I thought I must to get the best performance.' She explained this to the British team coach, Ernst Bachinger and headed off (somewhat suprisingly for a dressage rider) towards the racehorse gallops at Goodwood. 'I took him up them twice at a fast canter, and the next day I worked him for two and a half hours before the Grand Prix. That went much better. He was obedient and listening to the aids. It was a reasonable test and we were eighth.'

They had qualified for the Special, the individual ride-off, but then had the misfortune to draw first to go. 'I had only ridden the Special once before, at the Europeans. I had no guide as to what work to give him. He had been obedient but not at his best in the Grand Prix, so I cut it down and lunged him as I did not want to make him sore in his back. Then I led him around. I rode him for an hour, working mostly on the basics and then went to Bachinger for the last twenty minutes. Bill went into the arena and seemed to grow. Whenever I asked for impulsion it was there and he was soft and obedient. He rose to the occasion. By today's standard it might not have been fantastic but it was good for the dressage of the day. It was so fluent and easy and there was no tension; he was very submissive. He piaffed extremely well – Nyblaeus even gave us a nine – and he went from one transition to another very well. That is what gave us so many marks.'

Jennie was so green that when her score was announced she did not realise how good it was, nor did the enormous number of spectators who had come to see what this curious sport was all about. Gradually, however, as one mark after another was revealed and she still retained the lead she began to be aware that the judges had given her much higher rewards than ever before. The spectators too started to get excited as it became more and more obvious that a British rider was going to come out ahead of many of the Continental riders, who had been thought so superior to our less-cultured representa-

Jennie Loriston-Clarke and Dutch Courage in an extended trot at Goodwood.

tives. 'I did not realise how good it was until riders who had always beaten me, like Harry Boldt and Uwe Sauer, got fewer marks. The Pony Club kids who went to pick up the score sheets would pop up and say, "You've beaten another one!" Until the last two went we were in the lead. I couldn't really believe it.'

The Olympic Champions, Christine Stückelberger and Granat, and the European bronze medallists, Dr Uwe Schulten-Baumer and Slibowitz, did edge ahead of them, but Britain still had the bronze. Jennie and Bill were heroes and dressage was put firmly on the map of this island which had been so cut off from the sport's development on the Continent.

This success gave inspiration to many riders as it showed that the British could do as well as the other Europeans, even with the latter's enormous advantage of having dressage as part of their equestrian culture for generations. It made others realise, too, that one could not learn about serious dressage in England. Jennie had been on a six-week training session at Germany's National Centre in Warendorf, and that had given her a much better understanding of the sport. She wanted to go again, and with other leading British riders like Diana Mason, Tanya Larrigan, Stephen Clarke and Bar Hammond, she went for more tuition in Vienna under Bachinger. Everybody was eager to learn and turn Britain into a nation of dressage riders.

'Bill was much more established by the time he won the championship in 1980. His paces had grown and developed, and he had much more power. He got better and better, but other people got better too.'

Jennie was thrilled that year because she beat top German professional rider Georg Theodorescu, who was riding his very good mare Cleopatra. 'Bill gave me some very steady rides. He had become much more settled, more mature in his work. I never had to work him so hard again as when we rode for the bronze.

'Hearing the national anthem played for us was one of the biggest moments in my life, and to win in England made it even better.' They went on to win another championship in 1984, but sadly Bill couldn't make the Olympics that year. He had shown he was on form, and went well in Aachen, but 'he must have picked up a virus there. He was not well enough to make the trip to Los Angeles. If he had been there we would definitely have won an Olympic medal with Chris and Jane Bartle in the team.'

That Dutch Courage never reached the Olympics was one deficit in an otherwise marvellous career. In 1980 the British sacrificed their trip to Moscow to protest against the Soviet invasion of Afghanistan. In 1984 Bill was ill, and in 1985 he retired.

At his final party at Goodwood 1985 there were plenty of progeny who would follow in his footsteps and help Jennie win yet more honours. In the parade were his sons Dutch Gold, who was already competing internationally, Catherston Dutch Bid, who would win a record number of international Prix St Georges and Intermédiaires for Britain, and Catherston Dazzler, then a yearling, who became Jennie's seventh international partner. 'It was fun to get together the representatives of his offspring for people to see that he had been a working stallion during his competitive career. What a legacy he left.'

But on that day at Goodwood it was Dutch Courage who was the centre of attention and when Jennie rode him for the last time in the arena where he had done so much to boost British honour, there was hardly a dry eye as he did his final tour in piaffe and passage to the tune with which he had become associated – 'He's Got the Whole World in His Hands'.

His son, Dutch Gold, was very close to Thoroughbred, being out of a Thoroughbred mare. He first excelled as an eventer, becoming national novice champion, but his lightness of foot and his manoeuvrability meant that Jennie could ride him onto the beat of music and perform intricate movements. He became a star of music freestyles, which were only in their infancy during Dutch Courage's time. One year Dutch Gold headed the European League for the World Cup. 'Willow', as Dutch Gold was known to his friends, never won a Goodwood Championship but he did have the national anthem played for him. He won the music freestyle at Goodwood's 1987 European Championships (sadly before it was a European title), and he won the 1990 and 1991 World Cup qualifiers there. 'Willow rarely stopped up on you. It is a great assistance to have this in a horse, a generosity that will keep him giving you his best. Men can push the work out of a horse but women have to rely on the horses' good nature to oblige, and this is really an advantage as it looks better if the work is spontaneous and not forced.'

Having been the only rider to compete at every single Goodwood International Jennie has had a wonderful overview of the changes there. 'The standard of dressage has improved dramatically. Granat and Woyceck were the ones that were startling in the 70s. Now there are so many more. The quality of the horses is better and more people ride well. A lot of horses used to do some good things but had a hang-up somewhere. There was only a handful of horses that did a good piaffe in 1978. Very few got over five for a piaffe.

'The impulsion and collection is much more enhanced now. Possibly there is too much emphasis in sitting, to the detriment of the horse. We could be asking too much. We can see on videos that the old masters rode their horses much more freely, with less collection, but they still did good work.'

It is an extraordinary list of successes that Jennie has achieved at Goodwood. A contribution towards this was that 'everybody expects you to do well with the home crowd and perhaps I put more into it.' But it is also a special place for horses. 'There is room to move about, an indoor school, hacking country, wonderful stables and arenas that rode well. The general ambience was so good for dressage. It was beautiful but not over the top; there were not too many distractions. Most competitors had good rides at Goodwood.'

MARGIT OTTO-CRÉPIN

MARGIT OTTO-CRÉPIN and Corlandus hold the record number of Goodwood Championships as for three years in a row (1987-1989) they took the top honours and captivated the crowds. Margit's giant athlete treated Grand Prix work as if it was child's play. His soignée elegant rider never dominated her partner but allowed him to keep his spirit, which made him appear to be doing his dressage because he wanted to and not because he was told to. It was a formula that appealed to the British and Margit and Corlandus became two of the most popular winners in the history of Goodwood dressage.

Their wins included the 1987 European Championships at Goodwood, a victory that meant more to Margit Otto-Crépin than even the Olympic silver medal they took in the following year. She valued the great sense of occasion attached to that Goodwood victory. 'Goodwood was a real championship. It is the nicest place in the world, beginning with the stabling, and they have good arenas, the best grounds, super organisation and the nicest background.'

Margit had another reason for remembering that Goodwood as she was suffering from hepatitis. 'I should have been in hospital, not on a horse. It was like a dream-walk because I was not completely there. During those two days it was really Corlandus who did the work. He had to co-operate with me a lot. When I arrived in Goodwood I could not ride at all and he was lunged for two or three days. Under these conditions you do not forget.'

Remarkably Margit had had some of her greatest successes when suffering from this debilitating disease – she had won at Schoten in Belgium when it was just developing, at Aachen when she was really suffering from it and at Goodwood when she was starting to recover. It is recognised that for very determined people an illness or accident may not be such a handicap as it focuses their mind on what they want above all else; in Margit's case a European Championship was more important than her health.

Hepatitis was not the only danger to Margit's well-being, as the famous old oak tree

OPPOSITE: *Corlandus is famous for the great sweeping strides he could take in his half-pass.*

Margit Otto-Crépin, at Goodwood.

on the side of the arena nearly decapitated her. 'After the prize-giving we all passed under the tree and an American woman screamed. Corlandus started to buck and I thought I would get killed, my head was so close to the branches. When they took the other riders out and I had to go round again, he bucked again.' But Margit Otto-Crépin was the last international rider to have to duck down under the tree on the start of their victory round. Three months later came a devastating hurricane and that tree was one of the many whirled around in the winds, uprooted and left on its side. Many of the trees that were destroyed were irreplaceable rare specimens, planted up to two hundred years before by the tree-loving second and third Dukes. The dressage arena and Goodwood Park then assumed an entirely different atmosphere, a new openness and spaciousness, but at the same time it was more stark and deprived of some of the connections with its great past.

It was fortunate that neither the hepatitis nor the bucks under the tree caused any long-lasting damage and Margit Otto-Crépin was able to return in 1988 and 1989 to become a highly appropriate winner when Goodwood added another feature to its dressage. This was the lavish sponsorship by Hermès, who organised non-stop social entertainments with lunches, drinks and dinners all given in the style for which their stores and products are famous. The dressage was turned into the type of social event that had made the racing at Goodwood 'Glorious'. Spectators came because it was the smart place to be seen and not just to watch the dressage, but even the least horsey could recognise the appeal of the gymnastic Corlandus and his glamorous French rider. It was fitting for Hermès that for two years in succession their championship was won by the most stylish rider on the international circuit.

Margit might have had three wonderful years at Goodwood, but her first trip was not such a success. That was for the World Championships in 1978 and the driver of the French horsebox left the certificate of health at an earlier border and when they arrived in Dover the horses were put straight into quarantine. 'I was the only person who could speak English and I went into the office to scream.' Despite these tactics it was some twenty hours before they were allowed to leave Dover and they were still confined to special isolation stables when they reached Goodwood. Even the riders were quarantined, and after such a long wait some of the horses fell ill and others were very stiff. It was not a good start to her career at Goodwood.

Nevertheless it was still an important show for her as it marked the start of her championship riding. At those World Championships she represented France on Caprici, a French horse that she had brought on with the help of two French instructors. Her trainers had been Patrick Le Rolland, who was famous for being awarded a ten for his riding by Jook Hall, and La Doucette.

'La Doucette was a perfect instructor of what is written and I think that is very important. When we learn a language we

RIGHT: Margit Otto-Crépin receives her trophy as champion of Europe, from HRH The Princess Royal.

BELOW: Corlandus showing the high-class canter that produced such expressive medium and extended work.

Isabell Werth, the pupil and rider for Dr Uwe Schulten-Baumer senior, demonstrates a hallmark of his training – working the horse deep and low.

Georg Theodorescu, coach to the 1994 French team and one of Margit Otto-Crépin's trainers.

must learn the grammar. In riding you have to read, and that does not mean that you do the things the way they say. I have Steinbrecht with me all the time and if I have a problem I read it. La Doucette was very intellectual. He inspired me, he gave me the base. Le Rolland gave me the basis of how to ride in the collection which the French love.'

Margit Otto-Crépin is special, however, in that she has worked with a wide range of trainers, having moved from France, the old Mecca of dressage in the eighteenth and nineteenth century, to the current Mecca, Germany. There she worked with a succession of trainers: two were Otto Lorke inspired – Schmidtke and Templemann; then there was Dr Schulten-Baumer, who had benefited from Lorke's teaching via Templemann and by the writings of Paul Plinzner, trainer of the one-armed Kaiser Wilhem II. She also worked with Herbert Rehbein and Udo Lange, and most recently the 1994 coach to the French team, Georg Theodorescu. It is quite a list. 'I am very happy to have worked with all these people because I think everybody can give you something as long as you can choose what is OK for your body and what you can do. Klimke is one of my idols but he is a man, he has longer legs, and even if I work hard to copy I cannot do it.'

Margit has a great vitality and energy and enjoys a healthy appetite for learning: 'I love to learn. I love somebody who brings me new ideas. All of these periods with a trainer were constructive periods. I got out of them better. The basic line is always the same but there are small differences. I am never worried about saying where I got help.'

She found that the most difficult period was the one with Schulten-Baumer. That might have been due in part to having just made the decision to move from France and make her home in Germany. Until that time, when training with Schmidtke and then Lange, she had come for long visits but had to leave most of her horses at home. It was not a satisfactory situation long-term and she uprooted to put her all into developing Corlandus' talent at a new home close to Dortmund. 'With Schulten-Baumer I had to change a lot of my riding and that was very difficult for someone who had done it for some time in a certain way. I already worked my horses partly round and down but I did it in a natural way, and with Schulten-Baumer I learnt how to do it.'

Margit points out the danger to imitators. It is a subtle system. 'You have to work with Schulten-Baumer, not just copy.' Dr Schulten-Baumer, a full-time businessman until his retirement in 1993, has had the time to work with only a few riders and they have all been very gifted. The results have been spectacular. He has been the major influence on the 1981 European Champion, his son Dr Uwe Schulten-Baumer; the 1987 European Champion, Margit; the 1988 and 1992 Olympic, 1989 European, 1990 World Champion, Nicole Uphoff-Becker; the 1991 and 1993 European Champion, Isabell Werth, and the 1988 and 1989 European Young Rider Champion, Pia Laus.

Margit has followed his way. 'I like to put horses down to stretch, and my way is to work them deep. They need both, to work completely down and to work in collection. I like low and forward work, as well as the collected work with the double bridle, while repeating the movements of the test.'

Margit does not work her horses always low or always high and where she works them depends on where they give her their backs. 'My way of thinking is that they go over the back, in a good balance, round and from behind to the front.' One horse might have to be worked lower than another and where they should be worked depends on 'where we feel the back. Best of all is to do both, and I can do both. If you analyse Nicole when she works in for a test she rides them ten minutes low and then takes them up. Isabell goes up and down all the time.'

At her school, now at Gestut Walloch, north of Dortmund, which she shares with German professional, Van Laak Norbert, the horses all work in this alternating state of deep and low and high collection. To help preserve and develop that precious back, 'all my horses have five minutes on the lunge in walk, and then five minutes left and right working deep with nobody on their back.'

The other feature of Margit's horses is their character. 'I like to leave in them their personality, sometimes maybe too much.'

She admits, however, that some of that happiness comes from the horse being talented and therefore finding the work easy. 'If a horse is happy doing what I ask he has to have talent. To be talented he has to have the heart to want to do it and the body to be able to do it, but I put the mind before the body.'

She recognised the special mind of Corlandus when she first saw him. 'Before I saw him move, I looked at the exterior, the eyes, his behaviour, the personality, and then when he started to move I knew he was really exceptional.'

He had a mischievous temperament and was difficult in a test 'because I never knew whether he would be fine on that day or something would make him buck. He was different to Caprici, who, when he got hot he never settled again, but Corlandus, he would get calm again. He would get suddenly excited but then quiet again. He loved to put in a mistake. I always knew when he was going to do it! He would gulp before the mistake, and blow out after, and then everything was OK.

'He was able to do the funny things he did in the test. The ordinary child must concentrate in lessons, to listen and understand, but a smart child can talk with the neighbours, do something else and still come out better. For Corlandus, doing the Grand Prix and Special was nothing for him. He played with everything – the canter, the pirouettes, the piaffe and passage. He is so happy when he could do piaffe.'

With Margit's next Grand Prix horse after Corlandus, Maritim (her winner of the Intermédiaire at the European Championships at Goodwood), there has been a huge difference. She has had to make big adjustments. 'Maritim did not like the piaffe; he was not born with the ability to do it. You can bring out in a horse work that he was not born to do, but it is never such a pleasant picture.'

Margit has high quality young horses but this is the result of spending much time looking at youngsters, and then taking great trouble to investigate fully those she buys. Westphalia, where she lives, is famous for its industrial conglomerate, but also for the horses it breeds and the competitors who live there. Within an hour's drive of where Margit lives there are the homes of an astounding number of the best dressage riders in the world – Isabell Werth, Nicole Uphoff-Becker, Dr Reiner Klimke, Pia Laus, Gabriela Grillo, Harry Boldt, Monica Theodorescu, and so on. It is real dressage country. The horses are there, but you have to be quick to react to buy them. She travels around to farms and auctions with Van Laak Norbert to look at them but with so many people looking for dressage talent it is sometimes essential to move swiftly. Van says that he bought his best horse a few minutes after midnight – he heard about him that evening and got straight in the car to go and see him.

Many of Margit's horses have jumping pedigrees – Corlandus is by Cor de la Bruyère; Antares, on whom she was the 1993 bronze medallist in the German riding horse championships, is by Argentinus – and she sees many similarities between the abilities of the two sports. 'We need good backs and good liberty of the shoulders, and a big heart is what the jumpers need. The only differences are that our horses should be pretty and have good gaits.' This is where the horses in her homeland fall short. France has been breeding horses to jump with huge success but they have not focused on the paces, and the result is very few French dressage horses. Margit is, however, involved in a plan – 'Plus de Dressage' – which is recognising stallions for French breeding that could produce dressage horses, but she knows that will take years before they are competitive with the Germans. 'One day there will be dressage horses in France.'

The buying of young horses might be fun for Margit, but it is the riding of them each day that makes her really excited. 'I love my young horses, they make me feel so happy

The champions of Europe, Corlandus and Margit Otto-Crépin.

about each new thing they learn'

She bought Atoll by Archipel, the top-priced three-year-old horse at the Verden auctions and says of him: 'He has given me so much. Not in results, but the feel. There is so much propulsion forward, the three gaits are perfect and the feel comes into me. If I ride another horse afterwards I take them with me. People who buy made horses lose much.' They will miss the sensational experience of feeling the athleticism of youth.

The atmosphere at the school of Gestut Walloch is one of great dedication, but there is also time for great merriment, when the horses enjoy themselves and take off bucking, and for immense satisfaction when things go right, with 'braaves' and pats echoing around the arena.

Their yard has just a little flavour of French exuberance and chic, but Margit Otto-Crépin is very happy with her German base. 'If you want to find good horses you have to be where the good horses are. They are easier to find in Germany because of the auctions, and because they have real dressage breeds.'

Besides, she says, 'the main competitions are here'. The Germans have established such a lead in dressage through their breeding, training and competitions that it will be very hard for any country to catch them. For any ambitious competitor Germany is an unrivalled base for the sport.

EVA-MARIA PRACHT

THE PETITE blonde from Germany, Eva-Maria Pracht, was the heroine of the first Goodwood CDI in 1974, winning the Championship and Kür as well as the Prix St Georges and Intermédiaire I. She had been born to be a dressage rider, being the daughter of Dr Josef Neckermann, the first dressage World Champion in 1966 and Olympic medallist in four successive Games (1960-1972). He was also a very successful businessman, controlling the Neckermann stores and mail order interests and therefore able to have top horses and trainers for himself and his daughter. But it needed a very determined spirit for Eva-Maria to live with and up to her father's exacting standards. 'He was extremely tough and taught me with the highest of expectations. He was never satisfied and at odd times demanded the impossible of me. However, I learned a lot, mostly the utmost importance of discipline and obedience and never to argue while riding.'

Her own family was just as steeped in equestrian activities: she married Hans Pracht, a businessman and successful show jumper, and ran a stables firstly in Germany and then in Canada, turning out top horses. Their daughter Martina became an Olympic rider and in 1975 they gave Britain's future team rider, Ferdi Eilberg, his first job after he graduated as a *Reitlehrer*. When the Prachts emigrated to Canada in 1981 they built such a magnificent centre at Cedar Valley, outside Toronto, that it was used as the site for the 1986 World Dressage Championships.

That 1974 Goodwood Championship was a major victory for Eva-Maria Pracht. She beat the Olympic medallist from Sweden, Nina Swaab, and riders from France, Holland, Switzerland, USA as well as others from Sweden and Germany. 'I was extremely honoured, proud and happy to be the winner of the Grand Prix,' she says, and with this victory went a unique trophy of a horse and rider in a canter pirouette, sculpted by Lorna McKean and then cast in pure silver. Eva-Maria did not see too much of it as 'after my victory it was couriered to Germany where it was displayed at the German Equestrian Olympic Centre for the remaining year. I felt deeply privileged and moved to be the first competitor whose name was engraved on the trophy.'

To win it she had to do more than ride a good test. 'During the warm-up an announcement was made that there would be a fifteen to twenty minute intermission to

Eva-Maria Pracht competing for Canada on Emirage.

allow Prince Philip to arrive via helicopter and to land directly on the showground.' This presented her with a huge problem as she was riding a very sensitive horse. 'I was the next one in the ring. I had to keep a clear head and needed to make a decision as to what I should do with my horse. To take him back to the stables and then start my warm-up all over again would not have worked; to remain in the warm-up area and risk him getting scared with the arrival of the helicopter and then having to deal with his anxiety and tender nerves in the show ring would not have worked either. I decided to take off into the nearby forest to hide away from all the noise and excitement, and remain there until everything was over and my husband signalled to me to return. The

Eva-Maria Pracht and Van Eick winning the Grand Prix at the first CDI at Goodwood in 1974 before the sand arena had been built.

result was a calm and quiet horse, performing a beautiful Grand Prix test and then being rewarded by Prince Philip and Lady March with the great John Pinches Trophy. Some of my fellow competitors laughed when they saw me take off into the forest, but it was the smartest thing I could have done, and I ended up laughing when it was all over and I was the winner.'

This Goodwood show was a huge success for the Pracht stables, especially as the only international class that Eva-Maria did not win, the Intermédiaire II, was won by their resident trainer, Heinz Lammers. They were enjoying a great run of successes. At the Olympics two years before, her partner at Goodwood, Van Eick, had been the reserve horse for the German team and Eva-Maria had earned some great memories. 'The most important goal of my equestrian career was participation in the Olympic Games and therefore I will always treasure being the German test rider at the 1972 Olympic Games in Munich with my horse Mazepa.' Her father, riding later in that class, helped Germany to win the silver medal and in the ride-off took the bronze. As a finale to the Games father and daughter both rode in the Olympic quadrille: 'The crowning touch was being one of the twelve riders exhibiting the famous Olympic quadrille during the closing ceremony of these Olympic Games. This quadrille took place at night under floodlights in the main Olympic stadium. I will never forget that special moment.'

In the autumn after the Goodwood glories she was invited to give a display at the famous Royal Winter Fair in Toronto, Canada. Three horses were flown out to be ridden by herself, her trainer, Heinz Lammers, and Christilot Boylen, the top Canadian dressage rider, in a *pas de trois*. This entranced the Canadian spectators who had seen very little dressage. 'For my husband and I this was the beginning of our love and admiration for this fantastic country and resulted years later in us emigrating to Canada. To this day, I have not regretted our decision to move here and have had a very happy life, now as a Canadian.'

A year later she took another trip to Canada, flying out two horses for the pre-Olympic Games in Montreal. This time her second rider was Ferdi Eilberg, competing at his first international show. 'One of my goals and dreams came true when I won both the gold and silver medal at the pre-Olympic Games in Montreal with my two horses Van Eick and Duccas.'

The Pracht family finally emigrated to Canada in 1981 and Eva-Maria soon became an important member of the Canadian dressage team. She was a member of the team at the 1982 World Championships in Lausanne, the 1984 Olympic Games in Los Angeles, and helped them win their first and only Olympic medal in dressage when they took the team bronze in Seoul in 1988. She rode the Swedish Warmblood Emirage in Seoul and qualified him for the 1990 World Cup finals, but Van Eick, her partner in that early Goodwood victory, was probably her most talented horse.

He came to her stables in an unusual way. 'My husband had purchased fifty per cent ownership from Georg Theodorescu, but kept this secret and did not even tell me. A few years later my husband and I watched Van Eick in a dressage class being ridden by Georg Theodorescu and he asked me very casually if I liked the horse. I answered, "Yes,

Van Eick looks like a very nice horse," at which point my husband confessed that he was the joint-owner and if I would like to ride him he would purchase the other half. I was ecstatic and could hardly wait until Van Eick arrived at my barn.'

Like so many top horses he did not prove to be an easy character. 'Although a brilliant horse he was probably the most difficult and highly strung horse I ever worked with, and more than once I had a hard time staying in the saddle. He was master of the traits of being spooky, nervous, rearing and bucking - you name, it he did it! The worst, however, was that he could literally spook and jump away from anything he did not like.' That was the black side, but on the other hand 'when he was all supple and relaxed he was a star and a real treat to ride, which is what gave me courage and kept me going with him. Also his sensitivity and being on the edge made him into that extra special horse that you need to win in the show ring, such as at Goodwood.'

Handling top horses takes skill and bravery, especially for one so small and feminine, but Eva-Maria had the advantage of a top-class education in how to ride them. Her first trainer was an old riding instructor at the local riding school in Frankfurt, and then her father took over to instill in her the highest standards of excellence. Later she benefited from the help of the top coaches of the time: Bubi Günther, Willi Schultheiss, Walter Christensen, and, during Goodwood, Heinz Lammers. 'All of these trainers played an important role in my equestrian career and it gave me great pleasure and fun to work with them. Some are greatly missed by me, foremost my father, as well as Bubi Günther and Walter Christensen who have sadly passed away.'

From them she developed her ideas of how her horse should go: 'He should be light in the hand, supple and forward, with sufficient spunk to manage the high level tests, sensitive to the leg and, last but not least, intelligent. Above all, if you become friends with your horse he will reward you in the show ring by being alert to the aids and willing to do the best possible job he can. Hopefully this will result in victories for both horse and rider.'

She has bought many horses, both for the family to ride and to sell on, and she looks for 'three good basic gaits and large shoulder movement to be able to show off an impressive extended trot. Personally, I prefer horses with some nerves and spunk – even if that means they could get a bit out of control at times – rather than the type of horse that requires a very strong leg and needs to be pushed forward at all times. These horses with that extra little bit of "oomph" will prove to be, in later years, after all the training, the ones that can easily complete a Grand Prix test in the show ring without a whip.'

With an international career spanning more than twenty years at top level, starting at the 1969 European Championships where she was fourteenth individually on her father's Olympic partner Antoinette and continuing until her second World Cup final in 1990, she has seen some changes. The most far-reaching for her have been amongst the horses. 'It is my opinion that the emphasis in breeding is more now on producing specifically dressage horses, jumping horses, or three-day event horses. Naturally this does not only improve the quality in horses but also the quantity of brilliant horses available on the market and displayed in the show ring.'

HERBERT REHBEIN

GOODWOOD STARTED with a great champion, for Herbert Rehbein won the Grand Prix on Gassendi in that Friendly International of 1973. This slightly rotund German, born two years after the war ended, is generally recognised as the 'great' rider of his generation. He has not been 'the' great competitor, though, as he chose to become a professional, went through the demanding training in Germany to get his qualifications and was consequently barred from trying for a place on the national teams. Although an occasional competitor at the major German shows, and he has won the Hamburg Derby eight times, his considerable talents have been directed into training horses, competitors and future trainers and his trip to Goodwood was one of the few times he competed outside Germany.

He served his apprenticeship through the 1960s when Bubi Günther, the late husband of top international judge Maria Günther, was the acclaimed trainer of the day and referred to with a mixture of affection and timidity as 'zee boss' or 'god'. Bubi Günther was a 'magic' man who rode the horses of most of the top competitors of the day – Josef

Neckermann, Karin Schlüter, Ilsebill Becher and the like – and turned them into round, springy animals that with their owners back in the saddle won most of the major events. Günther was Rehbein's main influence although other great trainers of the day did play a part in developing his own individual system. He names the Swede Hans Wikne, the Portuguese maestro Nuno Oliveira and the German national coach Willi

Karin Rehbein in a very balanced half-pass on Donnerhall, the stallion who is making the stud at Grönwohldhof, near Hamburg, one of the most famous in the world.

A picture of beauty – Herbert Rehbein on Schimmel Container, by Condus. This top trainer of our time says 'Lightness – that is the art.'

Schultheiss as those who have contributed towards his approach as to how the dressage horse should work.

His career started at fourteen years of age when he was quick to realise that his future lay with horses rather than school. The first stage of his apprenticeship was with Carl Deal, who ran a riding school close to the Danish borders. There he show jumped and evented but was never in any doubt that it was on dressage that he wanted to focus.

He went on to work with Bubi Günther and then Germany's top lady rider Karin Schlüter, and at only twenty-two years of age he set up on his own. The year before, in 1967, he had proved his ability by winning his first Grand Prix.

He has been fortunate over the last two decades in working from one of the most comprehensive equestrian centres in the world, Grönwohldhof, north of Hamburg. Owned by Henrick Schulte-Frohlinde it is run as a stud, international training centre and dealing yard, and as such covers the three most commercial aspects of dressage. The facilities are unrivalled with two huge indoor schools, one of which is heated in winter and conditioned to remain cool in summer, hundreds of stables, outdoor arenas, and paddocks, and all in landscaped surroundings. At this centre great horses have been born, top riders have been prepared for the world's leading events, horses have been sold to become international stars, and trainers have been educated to teach others in their turn. The massive investment in bricks and mortar and horsepower has yielded exceptional results, but largely because there has been an 'artist' at the focal point – Herbert Rehbein has ensured that the top competitors would come, and that the horses' talents would be realised.

He trains in a way that has many aficionados amongst the Scandinavian and English-speaking nations. He has been Kyra Kyrklund's main influence, and he helped Carol Lavell from the USA develop the talents of Gifted for the 1990 World Equestrian Games and 1992 Olympics. His basic and very simple requirement is that the horse 'is easy to ride'. The horses are not held in place by draw reins, nor are they dominated by a strong contact and powerful aids. 'Lightness – that is the art. If I make the horse strong he is not so good for others to ride.' This approach has meant that he has been successful in the training of Thoroughbreds as well as the heavier Warmbloods. He claims that one of the best horses he ever rode was the Thoroughbred Dream Dancer and he adapted quickly to the more spirited temperament. 'He was very hot in the arena. I worked him in the morning then only briefly before the test.' Sadly, the horse died from cancer before making a mark in Grand Prix.

Critical to this development of lightness is the position of the rider, and Rehbein, never long on words in English, quickly homed in on the simple truth: 'From a good seat and good legs come good hands.' He does not try to 'teach' this to his riders. Few corrections to a rider's position are ever heard at Grönwohld; the learning process is one of absorption and example. Mirrors line the great hall so pupils are constantly faced with what they look like, and, more importantly, they are able to contrast it with what he looks like. When Rehbein gets on a horse he envelops it with his seat and legs and immediately makes obvious the real meaning of that well-used phrase, 'riding a horse from behind'. He is well aware of the importance of his example: 'When the boss rides in this way, the pupils ride the same.' He does little teaching as such: 'I do not say too much about what to do but, after some years and a little bit of talent, they become good riders.'

He does give some instructions and if these are not followed a pupil's attention may be arrested by a sudden deafening outburst from him, but his main means of instruction is by example and experience. The most commonly heard phrase is 'do it with feeling', and the best way of learning is watching him work the horses and then riding them afterwards.

At Grönwohld there are wonderful horses to ride, including those bred on the stud being brought on to sell and compete, those there to be sold, and clients' horses there for training. Pupils can ride-in the top horses for Rehbein and his wife Karin (a top

The great rider Herbert Rehbein on Gassendi, winners of the first-ever Friendly International at Goodwood.

international rider) and the best are encouraged to try a little undemanding piaffe, changes and half-passes before the great riders get on. Herbert Rehbein is well aware that 'pupils cannot learn without a good horse to ride. They need schoolmasters.'

Just like his master, Bubi Günther, his style of teaching is one of strong contrasts, with fun and music and laughter but vociferous corrections for those who have lost concentration; for the horses there is the occasional crack of a whip if they do not respond and an abundance of pats when they go well. It is obvious that he is right in saying, 'We work nicely together.'

Rehbein horses are light and easy to ride, but there is still plenty of power. There might not be so much emphasis on forward work as in other top stables, and the horses do not work so boldly or extravagantly. The development of the brilliance of the gaits appears to be of secondary importance to collection and softness.

Sessions include masses of transitions 'so the horse comes nice in the hands and the hind legs.' The Rehbein school does not practise the fashionable way of working horses deep and low as he says, 'Too many horses pull to the ground.' Yet although they are not ridden down they are often worked deep and behind the vertical. Roundness is very important to him. 'If they are deep in the neck they can come more over the back. When that is okay, they can come up.'

Herbert Rehbein's fortune is not only that he has wonderful facilities – he also has the talents to attract some of the great riders of the world to Grönwohldhof for training, and the breeding programme there means that the stud can produce horses of the type needed for his dressage. The star of the stallions is Donnerhall, whom Karin Rehbein rides internationally. This horse has won a mass of Grands Prix and has produced stock that is winning the Young Horse Championships in Germany. He is a son of Donnerwetter, whom Herbert Rehbein rode in Grands Prix and in 1990 was a finalist in the Hamburg Derby. Also standing at stud is Pik Primaire on whom Herbert Rehbein won the 1990 Hanover Grand Prix Special. Pik Primaire is a son of the late Pik Bube, another Grand Prix horse for Herbert Rehbein. The Grönwohldhof stables are building up a dynasty of dressage producers, aided by a very rigorous form of performance-testing for their stallions.

Herbert Rehbein might be exceptionally talented, but he is exceptionally lucky that he found an establishment which has given him the opportunity to realise his ability and spread the benefits widely amongst a very high standard of riders and horses.

SVEN ROTHENBERGER

❦❦❦❦❦❦❦

SVEN-GÜNTER ROTHENBERGER was the first top German rider to take the Kür seriously – and he has reaped the rewards for doing so, winning the World Cup in 1990, the inaugural European Championship for it in 1991 and the last Goodwood Grand Prix and Freestyle. He does not put his special ability in the Kür down to being more musical than his fellow countrymen: 'We have had very good musicians, like the composer Wagner. You have to believe in something, then you can do it.'

This is the hallmark of the Rothenberger success story: a businessman's approach towards the sport of setting high goals, systematically acquiring the tools to achieve them and thinking positively. Whilst Sven has had the good fortune to have the funds to buy top horses, he has also applied unusually strong determination and energy, which, when combined with a thoughtful approach to his riding, have ensured that he made good use of the wonderful equine material he has produced for competitions.

Although Ideaal was his first team horse at the 1990 World Equestrian Games, it has been the effervescent black Danish Warmblood Andiamo on whom he has won most of his glory, including the Goodwood Freestyle. 'He always fights in a positive way and is very good in piaffe and passage. He wants to go. The reason he is still good at seventeen years is that he is always positive. The character between his two ears is his main thing. It made me unhappy in the beginning but I knew if I could manage his brain I would have a good horse. He wants to go faster, to be better and this was a bad point for his walk.'

At the start of Andiamo's career he threw away many points in this crucial movement because he jogged and lost the regularity, but it is a special credit to his training with Sven that this pace has improved in their years together. Sven, however, puts it down to 'Nature and time. Young people like to think it is them who make it better.'

It is not just Andiamo's brain that has been an important factor in their string of successes, it is also Sven's. He uses it more than probably any other top rider to help him maximise his potential. At competitions he is often seen in a quiet corner, walking through the test on his own two feet. 'In the beginning I had talent but made mistakes in tests because of not being concentrated. I have learnt how to prepare myself.'

And Sven does not focus solely on himself: 'I think very much about the character of the horse. The way he moves. What he wants. The horse does not have to go the way you ride. I think of adapting my way of riding to the way of the horse. I am an amateur and do not have much time to ride, but I do have time to think about the horse. It is the reason I can ride so many different horses.'

He spends most of his day in an office and the three or four horses that he rides daily are worked between 6.30am and 8.30am and after work in the evening. He has to rely on help from the highly professional team that he has built up around him. First and foremost he is aided by his wife Gonnelien, who, as a team bronze medallist for Holland, understands the sport and is good enough to help him from the ground and on his horses. They work together: 'I rely on my wife always telling the truth and not giving diplomatic answers.'

Most of their horses are kept at their new home on the outskirts of Frankfurt, on the Erlenhof Stud which Herr Rothenberger senior has just bought for his children. Some of Germany's best racehorses have been bred there, and whilst the Rothenberger family plan to continue the Thoroughbred breeding, there are also stables and an indoor school for the dresssage horses.

Not far away, too, are the stables of Sven's trainer, Conrad Schuhmacher, where more of Sven's horses are kept and where Ellen Bontje, the top Dutch rider, is resident and can help with the working of his horses. So in this corner of Germany the Netherlands now has three of her top riders.

Sven had formerly been a mainstay of the German team, winning golds for them at

Working the horse in hand. Sven Rothenberger and Andiamo on the grass at Goodwood.

Sven Rothenberger and Andiamo in an eye-catching extended trot.

the 1987 European Young Riders Championships, the 1990 World Equestrian Games, and the 1991 European Championships, but in 1994 he switched nationalities making it easier to go to the same shows as his Dutch-born wife.

Sven first took to the saddle at an official riding club when he was eight years old. There, from an essentially non-horsey family, he and his sister rode the school horses, and did some vaulting, and it was not until Sven was twelve that the family bought a horse. 'It was not a dressage horse, but a very difficult mare. She educated my sister and me. She reared and bucked. We did not know anything about horses but we managed her.'

The first real help came when he was fourteen and the family hired Emil Konrad, a *bereiter* of the great German rider and millionaire businessman Dr Josef Neckermann. 'He [Konrad] was not a jumping trainer so we started with dressage.' At nineteen, Sven started to work with Conrad Schuhmacher and two years later was selected for the German Young Rider team and won the individual silver medal at the European Championships, where Rembrandt earned the first of his record number of individual titles.

Sven Rothenberger came to Goodwood to win the Grand Prix and Kür when he was twenty-five. He said, 'I was really impressed by the place and the tradition. It was a nice hotel, park, people and castle; everything was perfect. Aachen is hectic, but Goodwood was for the family.'

ANNEMARIE SANDERS-KEIJZER

ANNEMARIE SANDERS-KEIJZER was a teenage phenomenon who defied the rules of commonsense: she went off with her parents and, with little knowledge about horses, bought a flashy and totally unsuitable horse for her age, experience and conditions yet ended up riding him for her country and at the Olympics.

Annemarie was fifteen at the time she did this, and she had already won a bronze medal at the European Pony Championships in Sweden; nevertheless the five-year-old Amon was not a sensible purchase. As the family were to find out later, he was an extraordinarily well-bred dressage horse, being full brother to the 1984 Olympic Champion Ahlerich and cousin to the 1988 and 1992 Olympic Champion Rembrandt; in addition, his father, Angelo, was a racehorse so he had plenty of high-spirited Thoroughbred blood in his veins. Up to then she had only ridden small ponies ('I did not know a thing about horses') and had come to the Westphalian auctions with her father because she liked looking at horses. Her father runs a big transport company in Amsterdam and approached the sales in a more business-like way. He put crosses by those lots whose picture he liked, another cross if they showed off well in-hand, another if impressive under saddle and again when jumping, and by the time they got to the auction 'Amon had lots of crosses by him.' Annemarie still thought they were at the sales for fun, and only realised her error when her father put his hand up and bought Amon. 'My heart went "bong", "bong". I was terrified because I had never ridden a horse.

'We were so lucky then. Now we know so much more, we look for a horse like Amon and cannot find one. I wish we had bought him now because I have so much more experience and know so much more than twenty years ago.'

Youth's lack of knowledge of the consequences can be a big asset in the training of the dressage horse. Certainly Annemarie trained Amon to world-class standards pretty quickly. At seventeen she was made a member of the Dutch Young Rider team and won a bronze team medal, a year later they took the team gold, and in 1977 she won the individual bronze. At twenty she went to Goodwood for the first time to do the Small Tour at the World Championships, at twenty-one she won an international class at Goodwood, the Intermédiaire II, and at twenty-two, in her first year on the senior team, she came to Goodwood's Alternative Olympics and missed getting into the last twelve for the ride-off by only one point.

Amon got better and better and at eighteen he did an outstanding test at the 1986 World Championships. 'It was the best test of his life and he should have had an individual medal. It was nice, people coming up to say it was good, but it would have been better if the judges had said it. They should have given us more points but if the horse is old they punish you.' Nevertheless they finished fifth and were the major factor in the Netherlands winning their first team medal, a bronze. For most horses it would have been the end, but although Amon was troubled by leg problems and was not so good at the 1987 Europeans he was fit for the Olympics in 1988 and at twenty years of age produced a 'very good' test, although Annemarie felt the judges were once again hard on him.

Amon's long career must have been in part due to him having 'real fire, he would never give up. His training had to be quiet to make him relax in the head. He was a very good horse, but a little difficult in the head.'

Amon has been Annemarie Sanders-Keijzer's most famous partner and this picture shows how he could earn good marks in the piaffe.

She had to change her trainer when she started riding him at home after the auctions. 'My trainer was too strong. He was good with a relaxed horse who needed to fight to get expression, but Amon needed to relax.'

'He was not easy to ride. In a dressage derby it was funny to see others ride him. In the tempi changes it was a big problem. I could not train the one-times before a test because it made him crazy. He would run off after them and get very heavy in my hands. But as he got older I could manage him better.'

Amon had pretty unusual training conditions as his home was in Amsterdam in the corner of a parking lot of the AlbKeijzer transport company. There could be no gallops for him across the fields or walks in the woods, but one part of the urban facilities did provide him with a very cheap indoor school. A motorway bridge ran just in front of the sand arena where he worked. The elevated road was just over twenty metres wide and when sand was laid below, it provided a dryish, if noisy, area to work. Today, Annemarie's father has made it pretty smart, closing in the sides with wooden slats, but in the old days it was only the central area that was protected from the wind and rain, so the going on the outside track could be very wet. This was turned to an advantage at the infamous 1981 European Championships, where the arena was laid in the grounds of an Austrian castle and the going got deeper and deeper with an onslaught of torrential rain. The Germans, used to working in pretty ideal conditions, found it very difficult, but Amon coped easily with the going into which the horses sank fetlock high. 'For me, it was great that it rained. We were used to working outside in heavy ground. He made no mistakes, but still no medal.' They were fifth.

One of the problems of being in a city like Amsterdam is that it is difficult to get trainers to pay regular visits. 'Most of the time I ride on my own. My way is for the horses to work with me. I am their guide, and they must follow my light instructions. I do not have the strength of Klimke or Hinnemann, and they can train the horses quicker because they are strong and train more of them.

'I have been to a lot of trainers. From everybody you can learn something. Jo Rutten helped with changes, I worked a little with Harry Boldt.' But the one trainer who had the biggest impact was Ernst Bachinger, who was a member of the Spanish Riding School.

'I won a scholarship for a young person to help them train to get to the Olympics. I decided to go to Bachinger in Vienna and for two months I lived in a horsebox. I was there the whole day on my own. When I think of it now, I would never go back. But I had a dream: I wanted to go to the Olympics and would do everything to get there. Amon, Bachinger and I worked well together. In one month were doing piaffe and passage.

'Bachinger knew what they were asking for in the tests and what to do to get better marks, to go from seven, to eight or more. He gave me the details that helped to get the extra marks. I was always close to the medals and it is such small things that can get you the marks for a medal. You need to look at the details.'

Bachinger helped too with Amon's spirited personality. 'You needed to get tough

Annemarie Sanders-Keijzer and her Goodwood champion Olympic Montreux.

with him sometimes because when he is in charge he will not do anything. He needed a firm hand. Bachinger could give him that but when he said he was good Amon would run to him for sugar.'

Today Annemarie's top horse is Olympic Montreux, a horse that was already trained to Grand Prix when she bought him. However, she says she would never take this route again. 'It is difficult to ride horses that have been trained by another. He has his way and I have my way. We have to take a little from him and a little from me, but it takes so long to get it good together that you could have trained a young horse. We have had some big lows but are now coming up.'

Annemarie might have had problems with Montreux but she did go to the Barcelona Olympics on him, and she did win the Goodwood Grand Prix Special in 1992 on him. 'I always liked to go to Goodwood. The stables were so good. The only thing was the feeling when riding in the arena of it not being level. I know it was level but it did not feel it. '

Annemarie cannot run a string of horses like so many of the Goodwood Champions. She has a husband and two children to look after, and she does secretarial work for her father so she cannot devote her days to riding. Nevertheless there are still plenty of horses at her stables in Amsterdam. Her first pony is still there, along with Amon, who, at twenty-six years of age, is still very active. They are now her daughter's schoolmasters and when her daughter was just four she started riding *pas de deux* with Annemarie and they were such a huge success that their duet has been a feature at major international shows. Amon is a more difficult schoolmaster and has to be ridden in side-reins to stop him charging off, but Annemarie's daughter is certainly being brought up to experience horses in the way her mother did.

Annemarie has made time for one young horse who comes from the same breeder who produced the remarkable trio of Amon, Ahlerich and Rembrandt. She says, 'He is more difficult in the head than Amon but there is something in there that will make him a good horse.' She admits that the major thing that draws her to a new horse is 'the same as when you look at a man. You like them or not. The first impression must be "oooh". They must have that special something. If you believe in a horse then it is easier to make him into something.'

UWE SCHULTEN-BAUMER

᠁

GRANAT'S RUNNER-UP in both the World Championships of 1978 and the Alternative Olympics of 1980 was the huge Hanoverian, Slibowitz, but his very tall partner, the full-time doctor, Uwe Schulten-Baumer made his size less obvious. Uwe Schulten-Baumer eventually turned the tables on the partnership that deprived them of the highest honours, taking the 1981 European Championship from Granat and his great Swiss rider, Christine Stückelberger, by thirteen points.

Dr Schulten-Baumer had on this occasion opted to ride his second partner, Madras, the equally big horse that his sister Alexa had trained and on whom she won the 1981 Goodwood Grand Prix. He did, however, come back to Goodwood on Slibowitz in 1982 when he treated the crowds to some remarkable dressage from a horse that was in his eighth season in top Grand Prix classes.

Dr Uwe Schulten-Baumer and Slibowitz played a less discussed but equally important part as Christine Stückelberger and Granat in the trend for big horses and powerful dressage. The former's dressage seemed on first impression less expressive than the Swiss pair's – there was never any danger of explosions of energy, the control was always there and therefore the expression not so obvious. Nor was there the elegance of Marzog and Anne-Grethe Jensen (now Törnblad) who were their runners-up for the 1982 Goodwood Championship, but they had very special attributes which were the hallmark of very correct training. They were masters of gymnastic training and I wrote after their victory in 1982: 'Technically Slibowitz is outstanding, particularly in his transitions when his strong rider can concertina his frame into magnificent, shortened, collected strides, or long, extended ones which hardly seem to touch the ground.' Those transitions were breathtaking, fluent, 'through' and with the horse stepping well under the weight.

In the half-halts all Dr Schulten-Baumer's horses rounded and lifted off the ground, which are sure signs of good training. The doctor said there was no special key to these: 'They were the result of the daily work, but for me the main thing in dressage is to keep impulsion when collecting.'

Father and son Schulten-Baumer devised a system of training which gymnasticises the horse more than any other, but this was no pre-planned carefully designed development, it simply evolved as the family became more and more involved in dressage. Dr Schulten-Baumer senior started with some show jumping, but later turned to dressage. His son Uwe says mischievously, 'I was the coach as a boy. Father competed and I helped him, and then we changed roles. I began to ride his horse and that was my beginning in dressage. I competed very intensively from 1967 to 1985.'

He claims the reason he took to dressage rather than show jumping was simply that the best mount available for him to ride was an old horse of his father's who was good at dressage but not jumping. The success was immediate. This tall, lanky schoolboy had talent and soon found himself on the Young Rider team, coming fourth individually in 1974. Another horse was found for him, the three-year-old Palazzo: 'He got better and better and I rode Grand Prix with him in the early 70s.'

The end of an extended canter across the diagonal for Uwe Schulten-Baumer and Slibowitz, the Goodwood Champions of 1982. Note the clear positioning to the right, and the self-carriage and lightness of the forehand, which will make the transition to collection easier.

Palazzo became so good that an Italian, Fausto Puccini, made an offer for him and this was accepted, and the young student Uwe Schulten-Baumer was asked to go on a few trips to Italy and was able to help his more senior purchaser with his horse. 'It was quite an experience' – and productive as Puccini rode Palazzo in the Montreal Olympics for Italy.

Dr Schulten-Baumer was keen to impress that 'Father and I did it together; it all developed. When I started I rode at home together with my father. During my studies [in medicine] I kept my horses at Warendorf and around 1978 my father helped me only at the shows. Later he came once a week to Warendorf to advise. We managed the horses together and there was good co-operation between us.

'We developed our methods between the 60s and the 80s. Our horses – Palazzo, Slibowitz, Madras, Feudal and Weingart – all went to Grand Prix and there were more horses that did not get to the top. We bought the horses together. I bought Gigolo (later Isabell Werth's European Champion) as a four-year-old at Warendorf from a young rider. But that was the time I stopped show riding and I sold him to the sponsors for Isabell Werth.'

The Schulten-Baumers bought their Goodwood Champion Slibowitz at the Verden auctions. 'We only saw him trot up in hand. He was very big – 1m 75cms [over 17 hands]. It was not possible to see what he could do in hand, but the way he moved was great. At that time prices were not so high and we paid less than 30,000DM for him.' Slibowitz was a Grand Prix horse at seven, a team gold and individual bronze medallist at eight, and his successes became a major marketing asset for those Hanoverian auctions, helping to convince buyers that top horses could be bought at sales.

The Schulten-Baumers bought other horses at those auctions. Their best horses were Hanoverians.

Dressage and horses were major features of the Schulten-Baumers' lives, but only as a hobby – all involved, including Dr Schulten-Baumer, had full-time jobs. Family life was focused on dressage, with three fervent devotees – father, son and daughter Alexa who won that Goodwood Grand Prix. 'In the family there was always discussion and many debates, but never arguments.' Their methods of training horses were slightly unconformist – they did deviate from the

Dr Schulten-Baumer senior, the trainer who is the greatest exponent of the deep and low methods which have sparked such controversy but have helped so many of the top riders.

mainstream – but they have met with such huge success that many others are now trying to ride horses the Schulten-Baumer way. This involves working the horses deep and low, but, as Dr Schulten-Baumer was keen to point out, 'The problem is that most people work deep and low in the wrong way.'

The only other trainer to have had any influence on him represented another school, namely Willi Schultheiss, the national coach to the team and trainer at Warendorf where he kept his horses when a student and young doctor. 'He had the opposite approach to working low, but I used to get his tips and not his way.'

It is amazing that the Schulten-Baumers have had this success considering that dressage was only a hobby. The young Dr Schulten-Baumer could only fit in his riding between five and seven in the morning, or between eight and ten in the evening. 'But this was possible to organise when I was a student and during my early years in medicine.' The biggest problem was the shows. The growing professionalism of the sport meant that he needed to go to a show every second or third week, and 'the big horse shows needed at least half a week away from work.'

When he rose in seniority as a doctor he could no longer carry on his hobby as a competitor. In the mid-eighties he retired from competitions after nearly twenty years at top level, having started with Young Rider classes. In doing so he became the only Goodwood Champion to make anything close to a decisive break from the sport. Eva-Maria Pracht and Harry Boldt retired, but are still heavily involved in other aspects. This is one of the extraordinary features of dressage, that once hooked it is hard ever to get away from it. No other sport would be likely to claim that its champions from over twenty-one years are all still closely involved.

Nor has Dr Uwe Schulten-Baumer got that far from it. He might not have the time to compete but he still goes to watch the big shows. He rides one or two horses nearly every day and he has chosen to live in a house next door to the stables of his ex-team-mate Gabriela Grillo, so he can manage the riding with relative ease. He buys some young horses and then sells them mostly aged six or seven. 'The problem in Germany is that young horses of six years need the experience of going to shows. We have the system that you cannot start straight in Grand Prix. You have to start in the lower classes.'

He buys the horses himself and admits that this is easier than in the past: 'It is another thing to look for horses to compete and be successful with; now I look for horses that I like. I like a horse with some spirit, but not too much!'

His partner who made him the leading German for four successive seasons was Slibowitz. 'He was very quiet, very reliable – a fantastic horse. He did well in the passage and trot lessons. In the last years he had difficulties and I could not ride him too much in extended trot, but in the first years the trot, especially the passage, was fantastic. My difficulty was in the work with his neck. He was not easy to ride. He had a lot of tension in the neck in the beginning.'

Goodwood was where Uwe had some of his best moments with Slibowitz. In 1978 this very young partnership – nine-year-old horse and twenty-four-year-old rider –

emerged for the first time as the best of the Germans. 'It was my first big success. I was hoping, but not expecting it. It was an advantage because I was not the favourite and could ride more boldly. It is difficult when you are favourite.' Then they won at Goodwood in 1982, and this was the swansong for this great horse.

'Goodwood had a fantastic atmosphere. For us it was typically English – the arenas, the grass, all the people. The tents were like a market. Some of the people brought picnics, some were sleeping in little tents. Some even slept in the horse boxes.'

For Dr Schulten-Baumer dressage has changed since those times when he was at the top of the sport. Not so much, as some have said, with regard to style, but more in the type of horse: 'Granat was a different kind of horse to Rembrandt. The ideal type of horse changed after 1988 with Rembrandt, but there has been no real change in the approach.'

The test is over and Slibowitz is being rewarded in front of Goodwood House.

The changes have come because 'today it is a sport for young people of eighteen to thirty. Today there is another kind of system because young riders have better opportunities for training and to compete. The other thing is that there are more shows and riders begin competing early. If you want to compete you have to be full-time. This is possible for students but not later when you have a job. In Germany there are lots of horse shows but the main competitors are professionals or young riders.'

He cannot understand why dressage does not get more TV coverage, especially with the huge number of riders in Germany and the development of the Kür with its greater public appeal. 'Why don't we see more dressage? There is something wrong!'

CHRISTINE STÜCKELBERGER

ॐॐॐॐ

IF GOODWOOD was to remembered by just one partnership it would have to be Christine Stückelberger and Granat. Together they won the two highest honours that Goodwood had to offer, namely the individual World Championship (1978) and the Alternative Olympics (1980).

No other horse has had such an influence on dressage; and no one could beat him for a record five and a half years. During his career as an international Grand Prix horse from 1972 to 1982, Granat won both Olympic individual golds (one was the Alternative Olympics), two European titles, one World and a further three individual silver medals. For eight seasons he was either the champion or the runner-up in the annual FEI Championship. Such was his domination of the honours that riders and trainers tried to copy his style: they sought out the heavier types with big trots, they rode for more impulsion and more power, but they still could not beat him. The winning formula was not his style but his unique ability. His extraordinary movement was natural, and his power was enhanced, not created, in the hands of a great partnership, Christine Stückelberger, a highly talented test rider, and George Wahl, one of the best trainers of our times.

Granat's approach to dressage was thrilling to watch, and for many dressage riders their most memorable moments remain his half-passes. These were the epitome of cadence, with every muscle in his body appearing to work and stretch to its maximum to enable him to spring and glide across the arena in a spine-tingling movement. For the uninitiated who had never experienced the feel of riding a gymnasticised horse, one that can use his entire body to produce powerful movement, this might not have been their idea of dressage. And of the thousands who flocked to Goodwood to see the first great collection of dressage riders in England for those World Championships in 1978, some were bemused by Granat's success. For them dressage was about obedience, light aids, appearing pretty and doing the movements. The English thought of dressage as ballet on horseback rather than gymnastics and it was an attitude that at that time held back British development as a world force in international dressage.

What the spectators, the judges and even the other riders did not know was that Granat was totally blind in the right eye. Those infamous shoots forwards at a pounding

Granat, blind in one eye, was very nervous until familiarised with his surroundings. George Wahl used to do this by taking him on early morning walks.

gallop that we saw sometimes in the parades or when warming up, but more rarely in the arena, were the result of him being frightened.

Christine Stückelberger says, 'His main problem was when he could hear something but could not see it.' Part of their preparation for every show was to familiarise him thoroughly with all his surroundings. 'Once he knew a place he was calm and when we went to a new place we showed him everywhere around the arena.

'Everyone laughed at us but nobody knew about the eye. We told nobody as we feared it would be a disadvantage if the judges knew. We did not know how they would react, and we did not want to take the risk.

'At Goodwood Mr Wahl took him out at 5am on a cavesson and kept on walking him round. Schulten-Baumer was also up early and he looked at us and laughed. Everybody was laughing at us taking a horse for such long walks, but he needed to know everything about his surroundings.'

He really got to know the Goodwood showground and park in those long walks and 'that was why he was so nice in the test in the World Championships.

'With those hours and hours of walking I rode him for half an hour in the morning and three quarters of an hour before the test. It was one of our best tests. We were both really relaxed. It was good to prepare him not only in the exercise arena but also on the grass. It was lovely to have the opportunity of working that way.'

Christine Stückelberger had very special ways of preparing herself for the test. 'I am always with my horses, looking after them and I plait them myself.' On the day of the Special this made her late for the buffet lunch: 'I needed to eat, so before the test I cooked some spaghetti in the stables. An American looked in and he thought it was incredible that I was cooking spaghetti before riding in the Grand Prix Special. He wrote about it. But I rode well with my stomach full of that spaghetti!'

They won with a score of 1360, nineteen more points than Uwe Schulten-Baumer and Slibowitz. 'I could not believe it. It came like a gift. I was the first person to achieve the hat-trick – a European, Olympic and World Championship. I was really touched. Boldt, Klimke, Neckermann had not done that. Now there is Nicole, so it is two ladies.'

Goodwood, then, was the scene of this great triumph and her memories of it are good. 'I always loved the place. I felt so happy there, the park and the lovely ambience.'

This great partnership of the 1970s, and arguably of all time, very nearly never happened. Christine Stückelberger did not strike up an immediate rapport with this strange horse and on a number of occasions nearly sold him, and once actually did so.

The other partnership in Christine's life – with trainer George Wahl – produced astounding results in international dressage. He started helping her with Merryboy, a Thoroughbred, when she was just twenty-one years old. That year she rode him in Aachen and twelve months later she was reserve for the 1968 Olympics and the following year made the Swiss team for the Europeans. She left Switzerland and moved to Vienna, where George Wahl was the chief rider at the Spanish Riding School. There she could get the consistent help that she needed. Small and very feminine she needed a man to help her work her horses 'through'. Determined, strong-minded and a great test rider, she worked best when he was there to support her. George Wahl and Christine Stückelberger were – and are – a great partnership. Today, nearly thirty years later, they still work together on their horses at their stables at Kirchberg near St Gallen, where the indoor and outdoor schools nestle into the hillside. The horses can look out of their stables over the beautiful hillside farmlands, with the Swiss Alps rising spectacularly behind them and remaining snow-capped through much of the year.

It is a beautiful, rather isolated setting for the training of so many top horses, but in those early years it was done in the city of Vienna. From there they heard about the sale of some Holsteins belonging to the Prince of Magalow at Chiemsee in Bavaria. They were shown two trained horses that were too expensive, then into the indoor school came a three-year-old: 'He was very ugly but his brilliance was his expression. We did not know then but we heard later that they had two indoor schools. He was a little wet,

An early morning training session at Goodwood for the great trio of George Wahl, Christine Stückelberger and Granat.

Granat shows his exceptional ability to collect and engage his hindquarters in this canter pirouette.

but we trusted everybody. We did not realise he had been worked before. He had a quite fantastic trot, wonderful rhythm, and a lot more suspension in the normal trot than other horses. Later some riders tried to get the same from their horses, but they just produced more tension. It was not natural to them, but it was for Granat. He had incredible cadence. I have never seen a horse like it.

'At three years old he was ugly. His head was big, but we bought him for his cadence.'

Granat was sent to her home in Switzerland while she went back to Vienna to prepare Merryboy for the Mexico Olympics. Granat proved to be a big problem; nobody could ride him, and they even thought of sending him back. Then they found out the reason from a German woman who had worked in his previous stables. She said he was blind. 'We got a professor to see him and he said he was completely blind in one eye. After three months it was too long to send him back, but I wrote to Magalow Furst complaining that he had all my money. I could not buy another horse now and Granat was blind in one eye.'

Christine Stückelberger set off to see the ex-owner of her troublesome horse and walked up to the doors of the castle to be greeted by the Furst (Prince) himself: 'He was about seventy and so handsome and I was twenty and very nervous.' She explained her case: 'He is so difficult in his temperament and now I know why – he is blind. Now all my money is gone. The Furst did not know he was blind but he took out a cheque and gave me all my money.' Granat, one of the greatest horses of all time, cost nothing.

Establishing that great partnership and turning Granat into an exceptional dressage horse was a pretty hair-raising experience. 'He could suddenly be so strong. Outside he would sometimes take off. I never fell off him, but twice I nearly did.' It was not just the charges she had to control, but also the rears, and once he reared up to land on a wall of cement pipes.

There were a number of occasions when all agreed he was just too much for a girl, and a petite, feminine one at that. 'When he was five, still growing and getting bigger and stronger, Herr Wahl said he was a man's horse. We sold him to my hairdresser in Vienna and he came twice a week to our stables to ride Granat.'

At this time, however, George Wahl made the big decision to leave the Spanish Riding School. 'He preferred to go into the sport. It was difficult for him to get to the shows because he could not leave the School.' They left Vienna to move closer to her homelands and found a new base in Salzburg. They took with them four horses, including Granat and Merryboy, and the hairdresser now found that the journey to ride his horse was too long. He also wanted to build another salon and decided to sell. By this time Granat had shown off his brilliance in public at his first competition at medium level in Salzburg. A big offer was made for him, which Christine Stückelberger and Wahl could not match, but the hairdresser generously agreed a price with them that covered what he had paid plus livery fees. Once again Granat was Christine Stückelberger's, but yet again she nearly lost him.

She took him to Frankfurt for the Prix St Georges and Intermédiaire and in the former 'he did such a beautiful test, then, on the last diagonal, the arena was not closed by boards and in the extended canter he could see the gap. I could feel he wanted to go out. I looked at Herr Wahl and he told me to come out and retire.'

Once again George Wahl faced up to the fact that this was a man's horse and he asked Harry Boldt if he wanted to buy him, but he had seen what had happened. He refused and regretted it ever after. Granat was the horse that deprived him of winning gold medals, and with Woyceck he had to be satisfied with a run of silvers. 'In the years when Granat was winning everything he kept on saying he should have bought him as Granat kept on beating him.'

Granat had prodigious talent. 'He learnt piaffe in one week. Mr Wahl said he was so talented that he could teach him to do it on the spot in one week, and all without force he did it. That older Holsteiner line gave him the strength. He was so strong behind. But there was also plenty of Thoroughbred.' His grandsire was Cottage Son, one of the great Thoroughbred sires of Warmblood breeding.

He competed at the Olympics at just seven years of age, and under extraordinary circumstances. With no need to earn qualifying scores he was able to go as reserve horse with Christine Stückelberger expecting to ride her team horse of 1969, 1970 and 1971, the Thoroughbred Merryboy. 'It was only the one-time changes in the Grand Prix he could not do, but we learnt them on the big racetrack at Munich. Mr Niggli was the

Chef d'Équipe and he wanted Granat in the team. He had never done a Grand Prix. His first Grand Prix was the Olympics. His pirouettes were big and the zig-zag not so good, but he did beautiful piaffe and passage. He had not learnt the one-time changes when he left home but he made fifteen with no mistake in the Olympics.' Granat finished fifteenth in this extraordinary debut in Grand Prix dressage.

At Munich he did not impress everybody as obedience was not one of his high points. 'On the racetrack he took off and Hans Winkler and Hugo Simon (both great show jumpers) commented, "Stupid dressage riders, they cannot hold their horses." Then on the last day of the Olympics when I wanted to have a nice ride, we took Merryboy and Granat onto the racetrack. They galloped off and Hugo Simon was again heard remarking about those stupid dressage riders!'

It took some time before the judges really appreciated his extraordinary talent. 'At first he was not accepted. At Dortmund he was only eighth and eleventh. The Hamburg Derby [in a year when they did not change horses] was his first real success.'

At the 1974 World Championships in Copenhagen he came second in the Grand Prix. Prospects for even greater success in the individual test looked good, especially when a leading German bet Christine a case of champagne she would win. Granat's

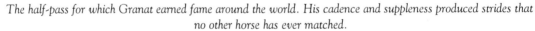

The half-pass for which Granat earned fame around the world. His cadence and suppleness produced strides that no other horse has ever matched.

weakness was the flying changes; that was where she made the mistakes and when advised to keep on practising them, that is just what she did. The problem was 'it made Granat tired. He made no mistakes but he lost the medal and finished fifth.' It is a lesson also that accuracy is not enough; it is brilliance – that knife-edge between explosion and excess of spirit with just enough control to carry out the requirements of the test – that the judges want to see.

They got it right a few weeks later in Aachen where they won four out of four competitions, beating the new World Champion, Dr Reiner Klimke, and starting their long reign of invincibility.

They were helped in this by the toughness of her horse. He might have been blind, but he did not go lame. Once again that old Holstein blood from the farm horses of the past proved its value. Granat stayed healthy after his retirement in 1982 and was ridden as a schoolmaster by the many young riders that were pupils at the Stückelberger/Wahl stables. He was twenty-five when he died.

His way of going will always spark controversy as some argue that he made the judges think too much of power and too little of lightness. Christine Stückelberger assured me, however, 'He was easier to ride than he looked. He was light in the hand. He had such powerful expression you thought he was difficult to ride, but he was light in the hand and quick to react to the legs. Sometimes he would get a little strong in the extensions. Others tried to copy his style but only produced tension. From nature Granat moved high and up. He had enormous cadence and suspension. It was the reason why we bought him.

'Today everybody likes to have a second Rembrandt. When I came with Granat a lot of people had Thoroughbreds, like Schultheiss had Brilliant. Then Granat came along with his great expression and power and when he had such success people all bought strong horses. It was not what I wanted. I did not buy him because he was heavy.'

In the first competitions the judges were not so keen on this big strong horse, but they were led by a great judge, the head of the FEI Dressage Committee, Gustav Nyblaeus. Christine Stückelberger said about him: 'Nyblaeus was one of the judges that thought about classical dressage, gymnastic horses and not getting tense and stiff. Many judges cannot see the difference between horses that are relaxed and expressive, and horses that are tense and expressive. Nyblaeus could see everything.'

MARKUS TECKLENBORG

❧❧❧❧❧

GOODWOOD 1990 was Markus Tecklenborg's first-ever foreign international show. The twenty-five-year-old economics student proved his ability by not merely winning the Championship with Franklin but also both classes in the Small Tour with the ten-year-old Preacher Man.

'The one week's stay in Goodwood will always remain in my mind. Not just because I won four competitions, but Goodwood was a wonderful event for my family and me. We enjoyed Goodwood from the first day. We had never before experienced a horse show with such an atmosphere with the stadium directly in front of the Duke of Richmond's house, the events around the dressage square, the spacious accommodation for the horses, the riders and their relations. There was a tremendous atmosphere amongst the spectators. They showed such a great interest and enthusiasm which especially impressed me.'

Markus Tecklenborg had been placed well in Aachen a few weeks before but this Goodwood show was his big breakthrough. Sadly it was not to last as shortly after the German Championships of 1991, in which he finished third, he was injured and unable to ride for two and a half years. Preacher Man, by the Thoroughbred Paradox I, was sold. 'His sensitivity and his expressive appearance made him, along with other qualities, a wonderful dressage horse.' Markus Tecklenborg used the time to complete his studies and get married, and in January 1994 Franklin and he returned to the competition scene. 'I had a wonderful come-back; we came fourth in a Grand Prix Special in Münster.'

Today he works in his parents' company and his job comes first, but he says, 'I hope to attend Grand Prix shows in the future supported by my family and my trainer Georg Theodorescu. I only regret that we riders have no possibility any more to start at Goodwood. But perhaps the Duke and the organisers of the show could think it over. I could imagine an invitation to all champions and up to third place with the motto: "The Champions Return To Goodwood".'

Markus Tecklenborg drifted into top-class dressage. 'The basis of my career as a dressage rider was laid in the equestrian club of my home town, Werne.' His parents bought him Franklin, a Westphalian Warmblood by Frühlingsball, in 1987. 'At that time we had never thought of being successful in Grand Prix but with the assistance of our trainer of those days, Mrs Heike Gratropp, Franklin and I grew into Grand Prix.

'It was a nice time: no one put pressure on us, and each step forward was a wonderful experience because nobody had expected it from us. Later when success appeared I had to learn to deal with the expectations and the pressure resulting from it.'

Georg Theodorescu had also helped Markus at an earlier stage 'in the transition to S-dressage'. His trainers' efforts were successful as, to quote my *Horse and Hound* report, 'Both his horses are examples of a free, forward way of going, showing lightness, self-carriage and an eagerness to do the work,' and 'he managed what so few can – a clear transition to collection, stepping up into it without a hint of shuffling back into a slower pace.' The training was very correct.

Franklin had the kind of personality which is common amongst the best horses: 'I call Franklin "my champion" because he is a real fighter and a very powerful horse. He always joins in, at work at home or at horse shows. Franklin is a horse that also has the will to win. He wants to win together with his rider, and he enjoys it. I really appreciate these characteristics of "my champion". It is not only the visible qualities of movement and appearance that are decisive for the success of a dressage horse, but also the will and the readiness to cooperate with the rider.'

Besides Goodwood, Franklin and Markus Tecklenborg won several Grands Prix and Specials, two Westphalian Championships, were third in the 1991 German

Markus Tecklenborg, who made such a remarkable debut at his first-ever foreign show at Goodwood, winning the top classes on Franklin (left) and the Prix St Georges and Intermédiaire on Preacher Man (right).

Championship and selected for the A squad of the German team – this achievement was 'the highlight of my sporting career', but sadly a career that was interrupted by injury.

The dressage was a family enterprise. 'I owe my success first of all to my parents. They have enabled my brother, Bertram, and me to practise dressage sports. They have always supported us in success as well as defeat. They have taken care of the horses and of the training and, what is very important, they have never put excessive pressure on us.'

Markus Tecklenborg rides his Goodwood winner Preacher Man in the practice arena.

ANNE-GRETHE TÖRNBLAD

ANNE-GRETHE TÖRNBLAD (formerly Jensen) and Marzog, champions of Goodwood in 1983 and 1985, did much more than simply win the 1986 World Championship, the 1983 European Championship, the 1984 Olympic silver medal and the 1986 Nashua World Cup, they gave inspiration to riders who favoured harmony, lightness and fluency and provided spectators with an aesthetic, appealing style of dressage.

Their successes were a turning point in the history of dressage, as through the 1970s and early 1980s it was the wonderfully powerful and gymnastic horses that were winning, with a form of dressage that thrilled the experts. The laymen, however, found it harder to appreciate, encouraging as it did strong riding. Marzog's dressage might have been less brilliant, but it had more general appeal and did much to increase the popularity of dressage amongst riders and non-riders alike, especially in Anglo-Saxon countries where this style was more in line with their less disciplined and more forward-going approach to horsemanship.

Goodwood was this talented partnership's first major international show outdoors. This twenty-nine-year-old Danish tax clerk and her seven-year-old Danish Warmblood had startled the Germans by winning the Intermédiaire II at the 1980 Dortmund indoor show. Then a few weeks later at the spring Goodwood, I remember chasing after the pair when they completed their first test to try and find out more about them. I had been captivated by the ease with which this bay horse worked, his eagerness to do what his rider wanted, and the charm of their partnership. This was the form of dressage I admired, and the epitome of that elusive FEI directive: 'The horse thus gives the impression of doing of his own accord what is required of him. Confident and attentive he submits generously to the control of his rider.'

They did not earn any high honours at this Goodwood show, but qualified for their first ever ride-off test. Then at the second Goodwood show of 1980, at the hastily arranged Alternative Olympics, the world began to take note of this young combination. Against much more competitive company, with riders from all over the world, they qualified for the ride-off, finishing eleventh. They also earned their first medal, as the

Danish team took the bronze. Next year at the Europeans they improved to seventh, and a year later came fifth at the World Championships. They were climbing, but they still took the world of dressage by surprise when in 1983 they beat the maestros, the reigning World Champions on their home ground at Aachen. The Danish pair won the gold and the great Ahlerich and Reiner Klimke merely took the silver.

It marked the start of a great rivalry that caught the imagination of the general public – the duel between the powerful Germans, with their spectacular, disciplined work, and the young Danish girl who had made it to the top without large financial resources or a big stables, and who had stayed true to a fluent style and had not tried to produce the highly cadenced and powerful work that had been the feature of the medal winners over the previous decade.

Her success was a great boost for the sport of dressage as it proved that talent was enough to get a rider and horse to the top, riches were not essential, and that the judges were unbiased and rewarded excellence. Judges had long been harangued by the press and some experts for favouring that power-driven style, but with this result they had proved that it was quality not style that earned their marks.

Most exciting for Goodwood, in the year of that great triumph in the 1983 European Championships, the Danish pair had also been their Champions. They won the Grand Prix and the Special at the tenth anniversary show, and they came back in 1985 having added yet another major credit to their list of honours, the Olympic silver medal. In Los Angeles Dr Reiner Klimke regained the upper hand with what most believe were the best tests of his career.

In 1985 Marzog returned to Goodwood to participate in the first World Cup qualifier in Britain. He won all the classes he entered, and in the freestyle to music showed that his way of going, his manoeuvrability and lightness were ideal for a Kür. He could work in harmony with the music just as well as his rider, and it was an accomplished, highly professional performance that immediately made them favourites for the inaugural World Cup final to be staged in March 1986.

The President of the Jury, Wolfgang Niggli, expressed in one of his rhymes the views of many:

> It was a very great pleasure to see
> How good a freestyle test can be
> The test that Marzog showed today
> Was really brilliant I must say.

That summer they had one of their more unhappy experiences. As holders of the European Championships it gave Denmark the right to stage the championships, which they did in Copenhagen. Anne-Grethe was the country's heroine, their Olympic medal winner, and she was subjected to considerable media hype and noisy supporting crowds whenever she and Marzog appeared for a test. They did win the Grand Prix despite a number of mistakes, but in the ride-off for the individual medals Marzog never settled.

OPPOSITE: *A good canter has an obvious moment of suspension, and Anne-Grethe Törnblad's Marzog shows this clearly on the diagonal at Goodwood.*

The epitome of harmony: the horse and rider working happily together and taking the longer strides of the extended trot with ease. Marzog and Anne-Grethe Törnblad in extended trot at Goodwood.

The tension reduced his elasticity, led to mistakes and they slipped to bronze medal position; Reiner Klimke took the title and thus became the reigning World, European and Olympic Champion.

This relative failure was soon proven to be a mere 'blip' as in 1986, when Marzog became a teenager, they had their best season. They started by taking the World Cup and then went on to win their greatest honour, the 1986 Individual World Championship. In seven seasons of international dressage they had earned nearly fifty international victories.

This was a remarkable achievement for a rider who worked full-time and paid little for her great partner. Marzog was born on the little island of Mon in 1973 and was a son of Herzog, with the Thoroughbred Marcio as grandfather; he was out of a successful dressage mare. The breeders asked Anne-Grethe and her first husband Tony Jensen to come and look at him, and they liked him enough to take him away for a two-month trial. 'In the first month's training Marzog demonstrated a very good balance, a willingness to co-operate, an ability to be taught and, not least, a good character, so we kept him.'

Tony Jensen had ridden Fox for Denmark at the Montreal Olympics, but was now turning more to the training side and during most of the 1980s was coach to the Danish dressage team. He and Anne-Grethe would train Marzog in the evenings when she got back from work. Sometimes in those early years Marzog would be turned out in the field to relax, but he soon became too precious to go out hacking. Anne-Grethe found herself the owner of a horse for whom offers of a million pounds were made. She had no hesitation in turning them down, but she always took the utmost care of him.

By the time he reached five years of age they realised they had a special horse. He won his first dressage competition and after this was hardly beaten until he started international competitions. Anne-Grethe devoted most of her non-working hours to caring for him, spending about four hours a day riding, grooming or just leading him out to graze. This helped to forge a great partnership in which he worked so eagerly for her. 'We are good companions. I groom him and lead him about in the fields round our home. I feel very close to him.'

Marzog did not need to be put under pressure when he was trained. 'I always started very gradually and took plenty of time warming up. I walked a lot at first then began with an easy trot. It was always a pleasure to ride him; he was so willing to please. He had such a positive attitude and wonderful high spirits.

'He was a very active and willing horse and always tried to do his best.' This meant he learnt the Grand Prix movements in record time and is one of the few horses to have appeared on the international Grand Prix circuit as a seven-year-old.

Goodwood was fortunate to witness much of this illustrious career – his debut in a Grand Prix Special, a Championship win just prior to his great victory in the European Championships, and his first run in an international Kür with the choreography and music that made him the World Cup winner. Sadly, though, it was an injury sustained on the journey which stopped him competing in the 1987 European Championships at Goodwood and marked the end of his brilliant competitive career.

After his retirement he continued to give displays to music, mostly in his home country where he was one of their great heroes, but his most memorable performance to music was an unrehearsed one when together with his great rival Ahlerich they did a *pas de deux* which has been acclaimed as one of the great moments in the history of dressage.

The great rivals of the mid-1980s, Dr Reiner Klimke on Ahlerich and Anne-Grethe Törnblad on Marzog, in their famous pas de deux.

ANKY VAN GRUNSVEN

∘❦∘❦∘❦∘

THE MOST SPECTACULAR champions of Goodwood were Anky van Grunsven and Olympic Cocktail. It was their first international appearance together – she twenty-four years old, he eight years old, and they had only one national Grand Prix behind them before making the trip across from the Netherlands. There was much excitement amongst the Goodwood spectators as it became increasingly apparent that they were witness to the debut of the first pair since Matador and Kyra Kyrklund to have the potential to break the German domination of the individual medals.

This handsome chestnut stallion had the greatest freedom in his trot that most if not all had seen in an arena. When he went on to Aachen, Eric Lette, the Chairman of the FEI Dressage Committee, gave him the rare distinction of awarding a 10 for one extended trot; and Nicholas Williams, another Olympic judge, apologised to Anky van Grunsven at Goodwood for only giving her a 9 for a half-pass in trot – he said it should have been a 10.

Anky van Grunsven was not prepared for this extraordinary international debut. 'We came to give him some experience. I never thought it would be like that. I had not even hoped it would be. What I remember very well was that in the prize-giving ceremony in the tour around the arena he did such an extended trot that no horse could do anything like it.'

Cocktail shares the common feature of all great horses: 'He is a personality. First he counts how many people are sitting there and if enough he will start going. He is a show-off. When he goes into an arena he wants to be the big guy.' Her other horse, Olympic Bonfire, on whom she was fourth at the Olympics, 'is much more nervous and shy'.

Cocktail's huge talent was nearly lost to the dressage world when, in the summer of 1993, a virus hit the stables, and it was of a strain whose muted symptoms were difficult to recognise. A slight loss of appetite was normal for Cocktail, who was routinely given as much food as he could eat to help give him the condition needed to combine his breeding and competition careers. After a training session during the international show in Rotterdam his pulse suddenly went up to 180. Cocktail was rushed to a veterinary hospital and it took three days for him to return to normal. To ensure against any recurrence, this near fatality was followed by months of rest and further months and months of very gradual increases to his work to make him fit again.

Cocktail is still Anky's second horse as it is the year older Bonfire who has been her team horse. Ironically she came to that 1992 Goodwood to concentrate on Bonfire as the Dutch were using the show as their selection trials for the Barcelona Olympics. 'I had hoped that Bonfire would win, but he bucked everywhere. He went badly and people started saying take Cocktail to the Olympics. He had lots of talent but he was very green.' Bonfire, however, learnt to settle better as the season progressed and in the heat of Barcelona his energy was a bonus. Anky was the highest placed non-German rider, finishing fourth.

This was her second Olympics, and she is yet another rider who took a horse bought for her as a youngster to the ultimate occasion for athletes. Hers was an even more unlikely case, as Prisco was a 15.2hh Thoroughbred, whom she had acquired when she was twelve years of age and to go show jumping, not for dressage. He was, however, so difficult that her father would not let her compete until she established more control on the flat. She was forced to make dressage her first priority and five years later she represented her country; and three years after this, at just twenty years of age, she found herself riding him at the Olympics.

Anky van Grunsven was brought up with horses: 'My dad did dressage, he was my first teacher. My brothers are show jumpers. All the family rides except my mum, and she does the laundry! My first pony is still with me. We did the jumping and cross-

Olympic Cocktail, the horse whose athletic trot and suppleness allows him to produce on a twenty-metre circle an extension that most horses can match only on the straight.

Anky van Grunsven on Olympic Bonfire, the horse on which she finished fourth at the 1992 Olympics, but who misbehaved on his trip to Goodwood.

country and we had to do the dressage.' Prisco changed all that, but only because he was so difficult and that Anky was brought up according to the Continental view on riding that the jumping could only develop when the horse could be kept balanced and controlled on the flat.

'It was the best lesson I could have had to start with Prisco He was so unbelievably difficult. It took so long in the beginning.' She really learnt to master those crucial basics of dressage and also to value Thoroughbred blood. Cocktail is three-eighths Thoroughbred, and Bonfire has a Thoroughbred dam. 'The Thoroughbred is difficult at the start but when you ride Grand Prix there is no problem in making the horse go. Other horses get tired but Prisco and Bonfire are only just getting going at the end of the test. I like horses that are a little jumpy. That is why I like Thoroughbreds.'

It is interesting that the commonly-held defect of Thoroughbreds – that they lack rhythm to their paces – is to Anky an asset. 'When they are too much in a rhythm it is sometimes so difficult to get them out of that, it is difficult to make them quick and sensitive.'

Prisco was the first horse to take her to Goodwood when she was just seventeen and a member of the Dutch Young Rider team. She came to the Young Riders CDA there and remembered one of her prizes was a white whip – 'but I never used a whip'. Prisco did not need any assistance to make him go forward. She was in that Young Rider team for three consecutive years but 'Prisco was not good at Prix St Georges'. It was Grand Prix in which he made his mark, and at twenty, when still eligible for the European Young Riders Championships, she went instead to Seoul Olympics. She also qualified for two successive World Cup finals, in 1989 and 1990.

It was her father and then Holland's Young Rider national coach, Jo Willems, who were her major influences as a teenager, but she admired the riding of Sjef Janssen whose horse President 'looked like a Thoroughbred. It had a nice way of trotting. I saw he could make horses loose and train all his horses to have an unbelievable trot and passage. I was used to riding a decent test, going deep into the corners and that sort of thing, but Sjef made his tests look spectacular'.

Sjef Janssen became her trainer and today they have a successful business south east of s'Hertogenbosch, at Erp, buying, training, selling and competing horses, as well as teaching. Sjef has an individual approach, although he has worked with the Netherlands' maestro Jo Rutten and with Jo Hinnemann from Germany. 'He reads a lot of old-fashioned writers and is always picking up ideas. He is a real thinker with the horses. We pick out horses and can see something in them and know the way we can train them to make them good.'

Their special formula produces that rare combination of horses that work with great forward zest and have tremendous elasticity and suppleness. It makes the horse look brilliant and maximises their ability. Most riders/trainers can achieve one or the other of these features but because forwardness usually creates a tension that produces stiffness, it is rare to consistently see both at the same time. Sjef Janssen's means of achieving what can easily become contradictory aims, is to work his horses round and often behind the vertical. 'It is a little bit like Schulten-Baumer. We keep our horses round and sometimes short in the neck, sometimes long, sometimes overbent, and very attentive to them being in front of the legs, seat, and so forth. But every horse is different. There is a line to the system but we change it a little with each horse.'

The real test of the system 'is to go in the arena when the judges are there and the horses do not go too deep. I see many people who do not train their horses deep but they go deep in the arena.'

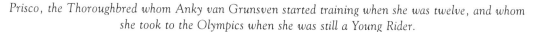

Prisco, the Thoroughbred whom Anky van Grunsven started training when she was twelve, and whom she took to the Olympics when she was still a Young Rider.

Anky warns of the dangers: 'Do not ride deep when you do not know what it is. You have to know how to do it. Keep your hands off that system if you do not know how to do it.'

Anky van Grunsven passes on her knowledge of the system to her pupils that she teaches in the afternoons. Her fun, though, is the mornings when she rides eight horses, seven days a week. 'I like riding every day. Riding is always fun.'

Sjef Janssen focuses on the training and marketing of the horses. He limits his instructing but says that he really enjoys teaching young riders, from just five or six years old and until they hit the teens.

Children are catered for in a number of ways at these leading competition stables, as there is even a play pen in the coffee bar that overlooks the indoor ring. Their large indoor school and stables is unusual for Continental Europe because it is located in the midst of the countryside, at the end of a lane, and there are signs of plenty of competitive-minded neighbours with several dressage arenas laid out in the fields.

There are horses in many of the fields in this area and it is a centre of the Netherlands' successful competition-horse industry. The stud of the breeder and owner of Olympic Cocktail is just three kilometres away. He first asked Anky van Grunsven to ride Cocktail when the horse was five, in the dressage competitions for stallions that are run through the winter and are important proving grounds for their stud career. 'I wanted to learn a lot more about riding and the more horses you ride the more you learn. I liked him because of his expression. The canter was difficult but there was something extra.'

In 1990 they won the National Stallion Dressage Competition so convincingly that they attracted attention and Anky was given the chance to train him up to Grand Prix. He is still used as a breeding stallion through AI, but with a very high service fee of 3,000 Dutch Guilders so there are not too many mares (50 to 60) and he can concentrate on becoming a dressage star. 'He produces really nice horses'. His first crops have been good enough for two sons to be graded as approved stallions, and they could well be jumpers as well as dressage horses. His pedigree is full of jumping lines, with his grandfather being Furioso II, the son of the most prolific Thoroughbred sire of show jumpers of all time, Furioso. There is also plenty of Holstein (a specialist show jumping Warmblood) with the stallions Martell and further back Antonio.

One of Cocktail's sons, Hocarlos, had, like his father, a major success at Goodwood winning the Magnolia Mouldings Potential International Dressage Horse Class at the last National Championships at Goodwood, in 1993.

Anky van Grunsven loved her trips to this Sussex showground. 'I was always really impressed – the stables and the house, and the really nice atmosphere. As it was in a field it seemed more like a vacation than a real show.'

THE
GOODWOOD DRESSAGE
STORY

Tineke Bartels and her highly strung mare Olympic Barbria provided plenty of excitement on their victory parade at the twenty-first Goodwood.

Goodwood's International Impact and the Freestyle to Music

❧❧❧

Goodwood set new standards of excellence in the running of an international show. Their entire focus was on dressage; no attempts were made to run show jumping and non-equestrian crowd-attracting activities. The competitors greatly appreciated being the centre of attention and the trainers showed how much they valued it by awarding Goodwood the first-ever trophy for the best run event.

Organisers looked to Goodwood as a standard maker and it was a natural step that the Duke of Richmond should become the first Chairman of the Association of International Dressage Event Organisers.

The international judges eagerly sought an invitation to judge and stay in this stately home. Wolfgang Niggli, for many years chairman of the FEI Dressage Committee, summed up their views in one of his rhymes:

For the judges it is clear
It is like in paradise here.
They can really concentrate
Afterwards they do debate
Whether the marks they gave were good,
What a rider better do should
Which horse was too much on the bit
And which rider did badly sit.
Whether a horse was correctly bent
Or only straight from X to A went.
This is dressage as it should be
It's success, you all can see.

Mr Niggli's description of his own first visit gives a little insight into how it was viewed on the Continent.

'When I was first invited to Goodwood I was a little bit afraid. I received a letter from the Earl and Countess. It was quite a problem to me to know how to answer. I called the British Consul to find out how to reply, how I should address them.

'When I arrived, my room was in the house of the [late] Duke and Duchess. Me, a little Swiss peasant, and now I was practically with royalty. I immediately recognised it was uncomplicated and within a short time felt absolutely at home.'

It is, however, Goodwood's role in the establishment of music freestyle classes that assures it a place in the history of international dressage. Goodwood was bold enough to stage the first international music freestyle, innovative enough to experiment with different formats, and confident enough to keep promoting it despite diffident attitudes from some of the competitors and accusations from some of the establishment that the freestyle to music was taking dressage away from the classical and towards the circus.

Yet dressage to music was classical. It was the form of dressage used in the courts of Europe, firstly in Italy in the seventeenth century, then in France and thence around Europe in great centres like Vienna. What was new was connecting it to the twentieth-century form of dressage – the competition. Freestyles without music had been run as far back as 1933, when there is an account of Richard Watjen and Felix Burkner riding in one. They became a feature at many events in Germany, and Britain used them through the seventies, including at that first Goodwood Show in 1973. Incorporation of music was only used in non-competitive dressage and remained the domain of the classical schools of Saumur, Oliveira and the Spanish Riding School, although there had been a few dabbles by competition riders. Most notable of these was the German dressage quadrille, originally staged at Potsdam, but the idea was revived with the Olympic quadrille by the top German riders at the 1972 Olympics. Their performance did interpret the music but it was still only a display not a competition. At Goodwood, at that very first 1973 show, the Theodorescus performed a husband-and-wife *pas de deux* to music. They put the display together almost spontaneously, the Duchess of Richmond having hunted through her record collection to find something suitable. And it was not long before Goodwood merged the music that was a feature of displays with the technical requirements of competitions.

As for so many far-reaching ideas it was the coming together of a number of forces

John Lassetter brought his Lipizzaners to Goodwood where they were schoolmasters for his pupils and gave very popular displays to music, like this pas de trois.

that led to the concept. The first of these forces was the Duchess of Richmond, whose ambitions and training to be a ballet dancer came to nothing with the outbreak of the Second World War. After she moved to Goodwood and dressage became her pleasure, she kept wondering whether these two loves could be combined. She herself used music in her indoor school: 'I was always riding with music. Sword [her horse] had the paces to go with music. He was more of a dancer than a dressage horse. I found the ballet was so much like the dressage. The control of the rider is like the control of a ballet dancer. Riding, for me, was always the nearest thing to dancing – the rhythm, the teaching of the horse to be athletic, the centring and the control. But it was even more exciting as there two living creatures not one.

'We had freestyles. I could not see why we could not have music incorporated in them.'

Just as the Duchess' great delight was riding to music in the indoor school at Goodwood, so it was with Wolfgang Niggli, heir apparent to Gustav Nyblaeus, who held the highest office in international dressage as Chairman of the FEI Dressage Committee. Every Friday at Niggli's school in Switzerland they would play music, firstly for the walk, then the trot, then the canter. He enjoyed it and it reminded him of his first sport, ice-skating. As a young boy he had been a keen competitor but his sporting career ended through an injury; later he kept up his connection with the sport in two contrasting roles. He earned his highest income of his life with two-minute displays on his skates as an ice clown, and he became an ice-skating judge. It was an odd coincidence that while the Duchess of Richmond was hoping to establish a greater connection between dressage and music, the future head of the entire dressage world had considerable experience of the one sport that used music in a similar way.

There was another catalyst to the development of the music freestyle. The Duke of Richmond wanted to give the dressage more popular appeal to help reduce the amount of sponsorship required. He thought his wife's idea of running dressage to music could be the answer.

Hence, when he and Mr Niggli were sitting together in the large library at the end of five days of the best dressage Britain had ever seen in the World Championships of 1978, and berating the fact that anything after that would be an anti-climax, the music freestyle entered the conversation. They had to think of something that would give dressage wider appeal and to both of them the introduction of music was the obvious answer. Mr Niggli, as an ex ice-skating judge, dressage judge and rider, became the technical architect of the music freestyle. Goodwood, with its artistic traditions and one of the best dressage venues in the world, was an ideal place to pioneer this new form of dressage.

In 1979 the Duke and Duchess of Richmond wrote in the foreword to the programme: 'If dressage is to grow in this country it will have to be more easily understood and more generally appreciated by many more people who have never ridden a horse.

'If that is to be achieved dressage will need to become as much an art-form as a discipline. It is for that reason that we have for the first time included in the programme a freestyle competition to music.

'Thereby we hope that you and many others will thoroughly enjoy what you see and thus become dressage addicts!'

There was much more to this form of competition than the riders and organisers realised. For the first year or so spontaneous choreography and attempts to ride walk, trot and canter to the same music could be excused. But although the crowd may not recognise mark-losing irregularities in piaffe they could see when the horse was not in beat with the music and when the music chosen was not suitable for the horse or pretty boring to listen to. Gradually it

dawned on the competitors that if they were going to turn this new form of dressage into a sport with the popular appeal envisaged, they would have to work very hard on their programmes.

In that very first competition the winner, Cindy Ishoy, admitted to little pre-planning and simply rode the movements as and when the horse felt ready for them. Competitors had to be persuaded to give it a go and the Duchess of Richmond came to the rescue of those who had come without music by finding them some of her own tapes; but at this stage it could only be background-type music so that the different tempos of the walk, trot, passage and canter would not be too jarring.

Some of those who took it more seriously and wanted to use different music for three gaits were offered two tape-recorders in the public address caravan. The system was to use an assistant who would put on the trot music after the salute, wait for a pre-arranged signal from the rider, usually a nod of the head, and then switch on the tape-recorder with the canter music and fade out the trot. The assistant then had to switch the walk and trot tapes on the first recorder and wait for another signal to fade out the canter music and start the walk, and similarly for the final music for the piaffe and passage. This was all a trifle complicated and open to a host of things going wrong. There were plenty of instances of tape-recorders not working, the assistant putting on the wrong piece, or not noticing the rider's signal, but as with most pioneering there was a wonderful spirit generated by the amateurism of it all, and tremendous enthusiasm to improve. Mistakes were treated as mere steps on the way to getting it right.

Within a few years competitors realised that getting it right involved an immense amount of work. Gabriela Grillo, a musician and international rider who led the field in those early days of the music freestyle, estimated that to cover the work on the choreography, finding appropriate music and putting together the tape, took her more than eighty hours.

Competitors also found that the freestyle to music gave them a wonderful opportunity to be adventurous, use their imagination and show off what their horse was good at. In 1982 at Goodwood, Jennie Loriston-Clarke on Dutch Courage stunned onlookers with work that was much more difficult than had ever been seen in a straight test. She did a pirouette in piaffe and fifty-seven consecutive one-time changes. Today such movements are seen relatively frequently but they had a huge impact when first tried out in the arena.

Riders soon found more opportunities to try out their programmes as other show organisers realised that dressage to music was a medium with crowd-appeal. Goodwood took the controversial step of running a music class in the prime time of Sunday afternoon during the Alternative Olympics of 1980. The Austrians at the 1981 Europeans used it as a consolation test for those who did not qualify for the ride-off, as did the Swiss at the 1982 World Championships where there was a memorable step in the development of the music freestyle. The class was run at 8am and Gabriela Grillo dazzled a small band of enthusiasts when they saw for the first time a walk pirouette turn into a canter pirouette, all absolutely in time with the music. When she did it then it was magical; today it is almost commonplace. Those early years of the music freestyle did produce some great moments when competitors tried and achieved something that had not been seen before.

Some scepticism about the freestyle to music was derived from the difficulties in getting the tests fairly judged. With the artistic element, objective judging was hard, and special skills were needed. Mr Niggli said, 'Whether you prefer classical or modern music has nothing to do with freestyle judging. What is important is if you see a horse with his movements exactly in the rhythm, that is what the people like and that is what the spectators can judge. A judge for the freestyle must have a good feel for artistic performance, like in dancing. Those who do not like to watch dancing should not judge. It is impossible to train for freestyle. If the judge does not have the right feeling he or she will never get it. I have a lot of disappointment because of the small numbers who have the feeling.'

At first each test was presided over by just three judges, but in 1984 five were used for the first time, and this has been the norm ever since.

Also there was the challenge of choosing a format which would secure adherence to classical principles and yet reward the artistic impression. The technical requirements of the test have never been in doubt and have remained the same from the start, but there has been plenty of experimenting in the artistic division, especially in those early years at Goodwood. There were a number of adjustments as to how the artistic section was scored. In one year two thirds were given for this section, one third for composition of the programme and harmony, one third for artistic impression and interpretation of the music and just one third for the technical performance. This was aimed at helping the public to understand the marking and also to give more emphasis to the artistic side, which the competitors were tending to neglect. In the 1982 Goodwood programme Mr Niggli wrote 'The technical side is being too much over-emphasised, and at the same time it does not appeal to the spectators or to the riders. In consequence, most riders have so far developed little imagination in the choreography of their Kür and only showed the well-known movements in another order.'

With this new marking programme, riders were encouraged to be more adventurous and this was when Jennie Loriston-Clarke produced all those one-times to win the class, but some riders with poor technical performances were amongst the prize-winners and this was not thought good for the promotion of classical dressage, so the system was switched back to an equal divide between technical and artistic.

There was much discussion as to whether a judge could be expected to assess the technical merit at the same time as the artistic, even if he had the ability to do so. The Richmonds were very bold on this aspect, and in 1980 they asked the Olympic gold-medallist ice-skater Robin Cousins, separately from the dressage judges, to assess the competitors' artistic quality of expression and movement in interpreting the music. The next year they invited the prima ballerina Merle Parke. On both occasions these celebrities selected a winner different from the one chosen by the dressage judges. Their use encouraged the riders to think more about how to incorporate the music and the judges to evaluate their judging of the artistic section. Olympic judge Nicholas Williams remembers, 'It produced some fascinating results. One rider used a syncopated rhythm for the walk and because the horse was unlevel it kept spot-on the beat. The artistic judge marked the horse up and thought the technical judges very hard on it! Still, if Goodwood had not tried we would have still been wondering if it would work.'

Wolfgang Niggli was very keen to talk to Cousins and Parke after the judging. 'They said it was crazy as they had no idea what they were doing. They had no idea what the horse could do. The horse could not dance like them. You cannot judge fairly if you do not know what the horse can do or should do, or what the reactions of a horse are. We decided it was not a good idea.' Outside judges were never asked again.

Formats were gradually being devised and established, the equal divide between artistic and technical accepted, and competitors were becoming more professional. Through the early 1980s the music freestyle gradually lost its pioneer status, an image that disappeared entirely when it was

David Hunt (far left), Chairman of the British Dressage Group, talks to three official international judges who have been major influences on the development of the freestyle to music. From left: Nick Williams, Eric Lette and Wolfgang Niggli.

decided that a World Cup for dressage with qualifying events should be run, not in the main with technical tests but with a music freestyle.

The first to put forward this concept was Dr Reiner Klimke in 1981, when he made a proposal to the FEI Dressage Committee in Laxenburg. 'My proposal put more influence on the Grand Prix. A horse with a real mistake in the gaits could not disguise this. When the Grand Prix has more influence over the placings, then the walk, trot and canter would have more influence; and also guaranteed was the classical correctness.'

His proposal was turned down. Wolfgang Niggli was not yet Chairman and Gustav Nyblaeus and the committee believed it to be too similar and therefore too competitive to the established FEI Championships.

When the chair was taken over by Wolfgang Niggli, with his affinity for a more artistic form of dressage, he presented another set of proposals in Zurich in 1983. 'This was entirely different from the Championships and with this we could realise the demands of riders and not interfere with the Championships. Because I had been involved with ice-skating I called an international judge in ice-skating. We could not do it the same way because dressage is different but we were able to learn from them and I was able to make a proposal

Goodwood earned a reputation for quick presentation of the marks in the freestyle to music. Judge Barry Marshall and his writer, the Countess of Inchcape, register a score of 7.9.

which the committee accepted.

'A lot of people said this would destroy classical dressage, but it did not because the technical mark was the same as the artistic one and the World Cup winner could only be attained through a Grand Prix test.' In the qualifying rounds, and at the finals, riders had to do a good Grand Prix – in the qualifiers to get through to the music freestyle and at the final the Grand Prix earned points which were added together with those earned in the freestyle.

'At first we divided the artistic side into three marks to correspond a little to ice-skating, but we looked at it after a few years and we changed. It was easier to only have two marks, because then the judges could get their marks up quickly. Especially at Goodwood they made us show the marks immediately and this is most important for spectators to know the results immediately.'

Wolfgang Niggli is in favour of judges giving their marks quickly. 'You have to decide immediately what is important. A judge has to school his eye and concentrate entirely on the little picture and you are not allowed to miss anything. It is terrible concentration. There is no time to think of anything else. For all judging in dressage you have to have technical knowledge then concentrate on what you see, decide whether it is good, rather good, sufficient or not good enough. You have to distinguish between basically wrong things, bad mistakes and minor mistakes.'

This is all common to both pure tests and musical tests, but the mark that should take on far greater importance in the freestyle is that for harmony between horse and rider. 'It is not used enough. The judge should make a huge difference between the rider who works hard and makes the movements through strength, and riding that is light and you do not see the aids.

'A freestyle programme is, in my view, an aesthetic, artistic performance of the unity between rider and horse, observing the rules of classical equitation.'

This is the dressage that Goodwood wanted to promote, and through the music freestyles it did. In the words of the Duchess of Richmond: 'Dressage should help a horse and rider to form a partnership, not so much master and servant, with its element of force, but based on trust. You do not get the extra out of a performance whether across country or in the dressage arena, unless there is that kind of relationship. That is when the magic starts.'

The music freestyle might have enabled some horses to disguise weaknesses in their training and still win prizes, but never the top honours. There might have been too much emphasis on the degree of difficulty, encouraging riders to focus on intricate manoeuvres rather than the quality of the work, but these minuses are few in comparison to the pluses. The main well-acknowledged benefits have been in making the sport understandable and appealing to

The 1993 World Cup finals in s'Hertogenbosch – Sven Rothenberger shows the lightness and balance of his horse Ideaal, with this one-handed passage.

the layman, but there is another, less obvious benefit: the slow, osmotic effect of the artistic mark on the way of going of the horses. There is more lightness, harmony and fluency in the work of today's Grand Prix dressage horses. To quote a leader in *The Times* during the 1994 Winter Olympics:

'If what Torvill and Dean do on ice is deemed merely middlebrow show business, sport could do with more of it. When taken to its logical conclusion, all sport is absurd. But sport is more about emotion than logic. If other sports gave marks for artistic impression, David Gower would still be batting, Henri Leconte would always win Wimbledon, Severiano Ballesteros would win championships more often than he does, and Jeremy Guscott would be shimmying through the midfield for all eternity. And the sporting firmament would be brighter.'

Goodwood's innovation ensures that dressage's firmament is brighter.

GOODWOOD
AND BRITISH DRESSAGE

Goodwood has done much more for British dressage than hold international shows. It provided the National Championships with a venue that encouraged sponsors to put more money into the sport. It put into effect many new schemes, having the courage to experiment and the organisation and style to run them in exemplary fashion. So many of the features of the current British dressage scene – Joicey Trainers, Young Horse classes, Pony and Young Rider Derbies, Young Rider National Championships, even equestrian pantomimes – all started at Goodwood.

Goodwood's role in the development of dressage has been recognised, the International Trainers giving it their first-ever award for the Best Run International Event and the British Horse Society gave the Duke of Richmond its medal of honour.

THE EQUESTRIAN CENTRE

Goodwood's first major equestrian venture was in 1972 when it was decided to set up an equestrian centre with an opening to coincide with the first international show. Jennifer Stobart BHSI was head-hunted from a job in the USA to come and run it. 'My brief was to attract equestrian functions which would enjoy the unique Goodwood facilities: accommodation for around 90 people in dormitories above the stables, and boxes for over 120 horses that were only

being used during twelve race days, and marvellous hacking on tracks leading up to the South Downs Way. A new indoor school was built and I was to plan some cross-country schooling areas. We were not to keep any horses or staff.' It was a novel concept in the running of an equestrian centre, but one of the few of Goodwood's equestrian ventures that did not become an established part of the equestrian scene. Instead it was to be the more conventional concept of a top training yard, but with a very unconventional trainer, that was to finally establish itself as an integral part of Goodwood's dressage.

Getting the equestrian centre underway was nevertheless an important contribution to future ventures, and as Jennifer Stobart described it, 'Life was full of variety. I attended many shows and competitions around the country to spread the word of Goodwood's new plans and possibilities. I kept a horse and rode sometimes with Lady March or escorted Lord March on his cob. I became secretary of the Goodwood Horse Trials. We hosted the National Riding Clubs' meetings, the Golden Horseshoe Ride, and ran courses with Herr Rochowansky. The film story of 'Jenny Jerome' came for four days on location, each day supposedly in a different country. As equestrian consultant I had to line up a dozen horses for Lee Remick, Ronald Pickup and others to ride, their colours different each day to contrast Ireland with Paris, England with New York State in various spots on the estate.'

The dressage meeting of 1973 marked the opening of the centre, but with the success of the 1974 show it became obvious that the major focus for the centre would be hosting dressage. 'I would have had only an administrative role so when the centre changed its style I moved on with many happy memories, and returned whenever possible to see the Park gradually transformed into the great home of dressage that it had become.'

Goodwood did eventually become a training centre when John Lassetter and his Lipizzaner stallions, having lost their own centre through bankruptcy of the owners, were offered it as a temporary base. The Duchess of Richmond was concerned that he might emigrate to the USA and his expertise, acquired through training at the two classical centres of Saumur and the Spanish Riding School, would be lost to Britain. The three-month stay turned into one three-year contract after another, and John didn't leave until dressage events ended at Goodwood.

His five Lipizzaner stallions were an admirable addition to the stables: they suited the style of Goodwood and their displays added a new dimension to the equestrian activities. Some of the most memorable moments include the drama of those greys lit by floodlights, working in their long-reins or in quadrilles. But John Lassetter provided much more than spectacular theatre as he combined it with humour which has done much to integrate dressage into the British equestrian scene and end its reputation as an exclusive 'foreign' activity. Humour in dressage helped to give it a British culture. It started with Christmas pantomimes, which the Duchess described as 'those mad pantomimes. Behind the curtain there would be three or four stallions and everybody changing, but they led on to getting more humour into dressage.' Those pantomimes showed

the way for others who began to incorporate theatre into dressage, all of which began to make it a more 'British' activity.

John Lassetter took the humour a little further and in his demonstrations started to 'take off' various sectors of the horse world, from the judges to the novice rider. It helped the dressage world to learn to laugh at itself and forge itself into a more confident, more vibrant and closer community, a better base from which its competitors could be launched. Foreigners laughed too; the skits were such a success that John found himself doing them all over Britain and even at shows on the Continent.

John Lassetter is unique in being able to switch from a very stylish classical rider to a ridiculously funny person, and to add to this he is also a very good competitor and trainer with a special affinity with the young. At the most stately training centre in the world he was able to give riders without financial support the opportunities to realise their talent, and two, Kerry Allen and Sonia

Three who did much for equestrian activities at Goodwood, the Duchess of Richmond, John Lassetter (with his international partner Twister), and Charlotte Penfold.

Laura Fry, who first won rosettes at Goodwood when she was riding a pony. This is Quarryman, the horse who helped her earn a silver team medal.

Webster, became British Young Rider Team members. With Charlotte Penfold and the Duchess' backing, he built up a 'team' of owners, riders and friends around his Goodwood training centre; he also plugged a hole in the British dressage competition scene. There was a gap for riders just out of Young Riders and not good enough to take on the top seniors. They started, at Goodwood of course, the E. Jeffries Future Stars Festival for riders under thirty and the scholars (the champions who received training bursaries) from the first two years, 1992 and 1993, Joanna Jackson and Lizzie Loriston-Clarke, both went on to be long-listed for the 1994 World Equestrian Games.

The excellent facilities at Goodwood were also used for training clinics. In the early days it was Franz Rochowansky, the ex-chief rider at the Spanish Riding School who had chosen to come and live in England, who gave inspiration and help to many who came on his courses at

Goodwood. Then another Spanish Riding School member, Ernst Bachinger, also came to help the English develop their knowledge with courses at Goodwood in the late 1970s. These were a series of clinics for the top riders, made possible by the sponsorship of the Hinckley Group.

THE YOUNG

Major beneficiaries of Goodwood have been the young, as this age group found a champion in the Duchess of Richmond, who has always felt that dressage's future lay with giving youth the opportunities. She did have a personal interest as her youngest daughter, Lady Louisa Gordon-Lennox, started as a showing rider, but soon became interested in pony dressage and graduated to riding Tamarisk at the 1984 Young Riders International.

The Duchess and myself were organisers of the first show devoted entirely to the under-21s and there was great excitement when Pony Club youngsters suddenly found themselves riding into the famous international arena on their ponies. This was the concept that showed there was enough interest amongst the young for there to be a separate National Championships for Young Riders, and this was launched in 1982 at Goodwood, supported by Taylor Woodrow. Successful riders that year included Laura Shewen (now Fry) who was runner-up for the National Junior Championship.

Nationally the young riders now had their own show, but Goodwood took it further and in 1983 started an international event, a CDAY, with classes from elementary to advanced medium and competitors from Belgium, France and Holland. It was the boost the youngsters needed, the opportunity to compete against their Continental counterparts and to learn from their considerable dressage inheritance. It was very much more of a learning process than a winning experience as in 1984, when more advanced tests were included, the British were completely outclassed. Four riders from Germany, including Holger Münstermann with Flair, who went on to be a runner-up for the Goodwood Championship at senior level, won all the major classes. The French riders were also better than ours, and the highest-placed British riders were Lizzie Mead and Carrie Adams with sevenths. Writing then I said: 'This domination should not be taken as disheartening but a tremendous opportunity to learn how it should be done. If these championships are to serve their purpose and show the British how dressage should be performed, the type of horses to ride, the way of training and the methods of test riding – then we need to invite the best.' It can be no coincidence that three years later the British Young Riders won the team silver medal at the European Championships.

Perhaps they took note of Anthony Crossley's piece in *Horse and Hound*, written in his inimitable style: 'We still appear unable to see and to copy what is shown to us at Goodwood every year. But until we do so we shall continue to operate, with exceedingly few exceptions, as if we were taking part in an altogether different ball-game. Until our riders master the basic style we shall remain as vicarage tennis players appearing by mistake at Wimbledon.'

Nor was it just the top young riders that were helped at Goodwood. There were Pony Club competitions and Pony Club camps; Pony Clubbers were used as runners at the international shows, and there were Pony Club displays at some of the CDIs. Goodwood also created its own branch of the Pony Club with the special aim of covering the needs of the basic riders rather than those aiming to become stars.

Another venture to help encourage the young to try out dressage were the Derbies. The Dressage Group allowed me to run a Pony Derby at the 1988 National Young Rider Championships which was open to any Pony Club riders. The four best qualified for a ride-off on each other's ponies and

it was the first major win for Laura Rossitter, who went on to be a Young Rider team member and Talent Spotting winner. The Pony Derby was such a success that the following year a second division was started for Young Riders, and thanks to Sheepgate, who took over the sponsorship from Moneeka Fine Arts, the Derbys are now an established feature of the annual calendar.

The most recent innovation was the E. Jeffries Future Stars Festival, which (as mentioned) was started in 1992 and gave pony riders, juniors and Young Riders a chance to ride at Goodwood; it also gave riders in their twenties the encouragement to progress and an opportunity to compete against their own age group.

Goodwood has also been a significant influence in giving our most promising riders an opportunity to test their ability against foreigners and to be judged by foreign judges. There is no doubt that it was at the Goodwood internationals that our most successful riders suddenly made a huge leap forward and became established as forces to be reckoned with. In 1990 Anni MacDonald Hall's second places on Floriano took her into a new international strata. In 1991 Laura Fry and Quarryman were first given good marks by the judges. In 1992 and 1993 Carl Hester and Emile Faurie made their big jumps towards international stardom.

YOUNG HORSES

It is not just the young riders that Goodwood has helped. In 1981 it originated the concept in England of classes for young horses. These were to be assessed for their potential as international competitors and not just for their conformation and ride, as are hacks, hunters and riding horses. The class was confined to four- and five-year-olds and was pretty high class as it included future internationals Hans Christian, Dutch Gold and Prince Consort.

In 1987, running at the same time as the

Young Rider National Championships but in the indoor school, I organised Potential Competition Horse Classes for three-, four- and five-year-olds, sponsored firstly by Lloyds Bank and then by Masterlock under the leadership of Desi Dillingham. Confined to British-bred horses these classes helped to give British breeders a standard for which to aim and made it obvious to them that the competitors needed a different type of horse from the hunter or show horse.

Another far-reaching venture for young horses at Goodwood was the occasion when some three-, four- and five-year-old Hanoverian Auction horses were brought over to show the British how the Germans rode their young horses, how they developed the expression and brilliance of their paces and turned them into athletes. With Harry Boldt acting as advisor and Kalman de Jurenak as organiser, the demonstrations helped the British people to realise that there was much more to dressage than making the horses obedient and light rides.

CONVENTIONS

Another influential brain-child of the Duchess of Richmond was the Trainers' Convention which I helped her organise in 1981. At that time there was little cohesion between the trainers. There was no British system and there was little to unite them.

Joanna Jackson, the first winner of the Hermés Young Rider Scholarship and of the 1992 Prix St Georges and Intermédiaire on Lady Joicey's Mester Mouse, gets advice from her trainer Richard Davison.

All had learnt under different systems – some in Austria, some in France, some in Germany and some in Britain. They all had different approaches which they defended, and they tended to work in isolation. The Duchess said, 'I was fed up that they did not talk to each other enough. They did not share information and some did not go abroad.' Her aim was to build up co-operation and understanding to promote discussion and exchange of ideas among trainers so there may be a greater agreement and better knowledge of the main objectives and of the present deficiencies in British dressage. 'I was very lucky that Elisabeth (Joicey) picked up on it,' and thanks to her support over the following years the trainers do now have plenty of common ground and have become the strongest single group within the British dressage scene.

In their two demonstrations at Addington in 1991 and then Osbaldeston in 1992 British trainers have shown the cohesion of their methods, and the strength of their talent with a spectacular trainers' quadrille.

It all started at Goodwood House, where the country's leading trainers were gathered together for the first time, staying in awe-inspiring surroundings, dining together at the same tables and with the same service that is enjoyed by royalty attending the race meetings.

The formula was similar to that employed successfully by many businesses, i.e. short papers followed by group discussion interspersed with social occasions. The time for drinks and meals was as important as the more formal sessions, for this encouraged individual conversation in a relaxed and informal atmosphere. There were talks from Britain's first Olympic judge, Jook Hall, the trainer of the young Hanoverians, Kalman de Jurenak, and from the highly articulate international judge who did so much to help the British, Jaap Pot. This stimulated the finding of common ground, and a confidence in their profession. And music convention. It was held on the morning after the hurricane. The Park was devastated, with many trees uprooted and lying on their sides, some irreplaceable, rare specimens and some more than two hundred years old, supplies of water and electricity were cut, but the convention still went ahead.

The next convention that Goodwood ran was in less dramatic circumstances. Dressage was growing so fast that the Duchess recognised a need for forward planning, for ideas to be thrown around to make the most of the vibrant atmosphere within the sport. She invited the BHS Dressage Committee and its new Chairman, David Hunt, for a 'Think Tank' weekend. He had just taken over from Diana Mason, Chairman of the Group during the 1970s and 1980s. She had ably guided dressage through a period of great development and had made a major contribution to the Goodwood internationals.

The 'Think Tank' of October 1992 at Goodwood was the start of a big transformation in dressage, encouraging a broadening of attitudes and a good environment for creativity, enabling, in the following years, many new ideas to be tried out.

The Duchess of Richmond makes a presentation to Diana Mason and Prince Consort on the occasion of his retirement.

when Lady Joicey helped them, firstly by bringing over Dr Reiner Klimke for their second convention at Goodwood, then by financing trips to leading trainers and shows in Europe, they were transformed into a strong group. Known for ten years as the Joicey Trainers they are now the British International Trainers' Club, and Lady Joicey, having made her contribution to Britain's senior trainers, switched her help in 1993 to the next level of young trainers in Britain.

The next area the Duchess thought she could help was in the judging and approach towards the musical freestyle. There was so much that needed to be brought out in the open, to be discussed and analysed, to encourage a clearer understanding about this important development in dressage. More information was needed about how to produce the best music and how to put it together. Once again, Goodwood saw the need and set about fulfilling it, and in October 1987 the Duchess organised a

OTHER ACTIVITIES

International dressage was what Goodwood became famous for, but other activities also flourished. The Riding Clubs used the grounds extensively for area trials and finals and for the staging of shows. Long-distance riders ran their Golden Horse Show Ride there, and driving and eventing ran National Championships at Goodwood during the 1970s.

The activity with which the Duchess became most involved was the Riding for the Disabled. Goodwood has long been used by disabled riders but in 1986 one of the first Driving for the Disabled groups was formed. Kay Hooper, the wife of an Estate employee, who drives with the Duchess, was the main

Alan Doxey on Royal Star competing at the Shell Gas National Championships. They have won almost the complete range of championships from Novice up to Intermédiaire.

force behind this venture which makes it possible for persons who cannot even ride to become involved with the horses. They have twenty-one disabled members and meet every Wednesday morning in the Park.

NATIONAL CHAMPIONSHIPS

For four years the Duchess and I ran national shows at Goodwood to make those magnificent facilities available to more British riders. Margaret Winn was once again the secretary. There was plenty of experimenting, with international judges like Jaap Pot helping with training, those young Hanoverian horses coming over, protocol judging, freestyles, and special opportunities for the young.

These proved that riders were prepared to come from all over Britain, even from the far north, to compete at Goodwood and the

argument that the National Championships must be in the centre of England lost its weight. In 1981, after running the National Championships in the main arena at the National Agricultural Centre at Stoneleigh, in car parks there to give it more room, and at Solihull, it was eventually decided to try Goodwood.

For the first time the National Championships had an aura of importance, competitors thought it worth the journey, and the sponsors, Taylor Woodrow, loved the added splendour of the occasion. It was the company's diamond jubilee year and the seventh year that they had sponsored the dressage National Championships. That year they had sponsored forty elementaries, ten mediums, eight Prix St Georges, six advanced classes and provided rosettes for one hundred and thirty novice qualifiers. It was the first time, too, that the Advanced National Championship was to be a Grand Prix, which Dutch Courage and Jennie Loriston-Clarke duly won for the fifth successive year.

The National Championships grew in stature at Goodwood, and as numbers of riders multiplied, qualifications became increasingly stringent, starting with the introduction of regional rounds at novice and elementary levels and progressing to medium and advanced medium.

There were some memorable years, the first being when Ferdi Eilberg took the championships by storm just after he emigrated to England from Germany to run a Dalgety Scheme to help Britain's top riders. In his first British National Championships he showed how young horses should be trained, Continental style, and won practically every championship except the Grand Prix.

A similar lesson in the value of the Continental approach was given in 1988 when Dr and Mrs Bechtolsheimer's horses, in the hands of Heinz Schweistries, won most of the championships. Of the British stars, outstanding was Catherston Dutch

The trot up, with Carl Hester showing off Giorgione to the jury.

Bid, who as a five-year-old won the novice and elementary, and as a six-year-old the elementary, medium and advanced medium. Another to gradually work up the scales was Alan Doxey with Royal Star, who started off with the novice and elementary and worked through until in 1993 they won the Intermédiaire and Prix St Georges championships.

The most startling change to the National Championships was when Shell Gas took over from Taylor Woodrow in 1992. Inspired by managing director, John Tew, they gave dressage an entirely fresh approach. Grass-roots riders were given more recognition, there was more ceremony, more prizes, more hype, more fun, more parties, more demonstrations and evening entertainments.

The 1993 Shell Gas National Championships was the last major dressage event at Goodwood. The Duke and Duchess were moving out of the house in favour of their son Charles, Lord March, who would later take on the running of the Estate.

Sponsorship for dressage events, particularly on the scale required for the standards set by Goodwood, was increasingly difficult to find, and, as with every one of his ancestors, the new resident of the house had his own different interests. Although he rides horses, his first interest is in motor sport and he has run a hugely successful festival of speed, a hill climb for cars of the '50s and '60s, past the house.

During that last afternoon of top-class dressage at Goodwood, storm clouds hung overhead and increased the gloom generated by this being the last time that wonderful equestrian athletes would be dancing in front of the judges at Goodwood House. The tenth Duke and Duchess of Richmond and the Goodwood Estate had done their work. They had used their home to transform a classical sport, 'foreign' to the British, into one that was the equestrian sport of the nineties, the one that ever-increasing numbers of riders were trying out, and one in which our top riders had at last become good enough to win medals. The Richmonds

Emile Faurie and Virtu, the National Champions of 1993, were the last combination to make a victory parade, and they did so against a dramatic background of storm clouds.

have been the major contributors in making it part of the British equestrian culture.

The 1993 silver and bronze medallists and the National Advanced Champions, Emile Faurie and Virtu, were the last to go on a victory parade around the international arena. They galloped out of the arena, against a backcloth of rich, black storm clouds. The winds whistled. And although Goodwood was not glorious on that day when it said goodbye to dressage, for over twenty-one years it had made a glorious contribution to the development of this most elegant of sports.

APPENDIX
A Brief History of Dressage at Goodwood

1973

Spectators watched on straw bales positioned around grass arenas. There were none of the frills and grandeur that were later associated with the event, and Sothebys put up just £353 for the prize money for the three classes (Elementary, Intermédiaire and Grand Prix) on the third and final day, the 15th July.

The main arena and the practice area were positioned parallel to the road, directly in front of the house, and alongside them were two further small arenas. All were on a slope, but in those days even the international competitors were used to riding on grass.

Nor were the classes confined to the international tests and the range of grades catered for were from Novice to Grand Prix. In the opening test, a Novice, there were some who were still riding twenty years later, like Penny Goring, Gillian Drew, Barbara Hammond, and others who turned to judging, like Hazel Killick, Barry Marshall, Leonie Marshall, Pat Manning and Domini Morgan.

Standards ranged from Novice 18, which was sponsored by Calia (who sponsored the National Dressage Championships), through all the levels and included a German test of Advanced Medium standard. In addition to the straight tests there was a freestyle, but without music.

There was just one international judge, the late Jaap Pot from the Netherlands, and he adjudicated at every Goodwood International until his health deteriorated.

In the Grand Prix just three British riders took on the Germans, namely the late Lorna Johnstone, Molly Sivewright and Domini Morgan. The first prize was a mere £75.

SPONSORS: The George Bradbury Memorial Trust, Power Marine Limited, The Canine and Livestock Insurance Assn Ltd, Upjohn Ltd, Sotheby and Company

RESULTS
Grand Prix: Gassendi with Herbert Rehbein for Germany

1974

The FEI awarded Goodwood CDI status and John Pinches, the makers of sporting medals, coins and commemorative medals, came in as overall sponsors.

The arenas were still grass ones and it was once again a German who took the highest honours, this time Eva-Maria Pracht, the daughter of Josef Neckermann, one of her country's greatest riders and a business tycoon. In the Grand Prix she had only one British contestant to beat and that was Jennie Loriston-Clarke on Kadett. Her stables dominated the proceedings, with herself winning four classes and her trainer

The first CDI at Goodwood, when Jennie Loriston-Clarke and Kadett were the only British combination to take on the foreigners in the Grand Prix.

Heinz Lammers another.

There were plenty of lower level classes and an imaginative National Championship run at Medium level, which was a contest between the eventers and the purists. Horses qualified for this from a Medium test and a three-day-event test with the latter attracting all the big names. Richard Meade won from Lucinda Prior-Palmer, with Derek Allhusen, Bar Hammond, Hugh Thomas and Mary Gordon Watson being amongst the prize-winners. When the eventers took on the pure dressage riders in the final they were remarkably successful. Not surprisingly, Jook Hall won with her outstanding eight-year-old home-bred Abound by Abyss, and the five-year-old Dutch Courage was second, but then came Wayfarer and Richard Meade, who beat many good dressage riders.

SPONSORS: John Pinches Ltd

RESULTS
National Championship: Abound with Jook Hall for Great Britain

Prix St Georges and Intermédiaire I: Duccas with Eva-Maria Pracht for Germany

Intermédiaire I: Gasal with Heinz Lammers for Germany

Grand Prix and Kür: Van Eick with Eva-Maria Pracht for Germany

1975

Competitions were on a sand arena made possible by finance from John Pinches Ltd.

For the first time at Goodwood the Germans were beaten as France's Dominique d'Esmé, who had recently returned to dressage after being a show jumper and event rider, won the Grand Prix and the Lorna McKean silver trophy.

SPONSORS: John Pinches Ltd

RESULTS
Grand Prix: Reims with Dominique d'Esmé for France

1976

The Germans reasserted their supremacy in 1976 as they sent over one of their greatest riders of all time, and now their national coach, Harry Boldt. The runner-up was also German, Hans-Dietmar Wolff on Renommee.

The show was used as the Olympic trial by the British Dressage Group.

A wide range of outside activities were laid on to help attract the crowds. This included a driving event, Riding Club pairs and team contests, with national dressage competitions at all levels and driving.

Competitors in the driving classes, a relatively new form of FEI competition, included HRH Prince Philip who had been instrumental in turning combined driving into an international sport.

SPONSORS: John Pinches Ltd

RESULTS
Grand Prix: Cosima with Harry Boldt for Germany

1977

The side attractions were still a feature of Goodwood CDI with well-filled Novice, Elementary and Riding Club classes, and the driving attracting more competitors. The dressage for this was at Cook's Camp, the marathon around the glorious fields of Goodwood between the golf course and the racehorse gallops, and the obstacle driving in front of the house itself.

The reigning World Champions, Dr Reiner Klimke and Mehmed, won the Championship and gave inspiration to many British riders.

SPONSORS: Franklin Mint for the John Pinches Awards

RESULTS
Grand Prix: Mehmed with Dr Reiner Klimke for Germany

1978

This was the year that the World Championships came to Goodwood. The best in the world came to England and there was no need to have any added attractions. The dressage was the only activity. Spectators flocked into Goodwood to see what dressage was all about. Seventy-nine horses came to contest the honours from Prix St Georges level, which ran over one entire day, to the individual medal-winning test which was decided in the first-ever Grand Prix Special at Goodwood. Teams were sent from Germany, Russia, Switzerland, Sweden, France, Denmark, Holland, USA and Britain, and there were individuals from Austria, Canada, Finland and Japan.

To ensure the fairest possible contest, the specialist arena designer Herman Duceck from Denmark, was called in to build a level arena. Amazingly there was such a huge slope to the grass in front of the house that this entailed cutting well into the hill. When it was finished it created an optical illusion. Nobody believed it was level and the only way to convince them was with a spirit level. Press and riders watched Herman Duceck prove that the slope was a trick of the eye.

Britain enjoyed an unexpected success with dressage even getting onto the television news as Jennie Loriston-Clarke and hers and Mrs Steele's nine-year-old stallion Dutch Courage beat almost all of those visiting experts. The British pair were pleased to qualify for the individual ride-off but then had the misfortune to draw first place. With nothing to lose they were relaxed enough to perform to their best. One after another the far more experienced and successful foreigners went in and could not beat their score. Even Harry Boldt and Woyceck, Olympic individual silver medal-lists, failed to get a better score. Dressage had suddenly become very exciting.

Inevitably the very best did get higher scores, with Dr Uwe Schulten-Baumer and

Slibowitz from Germany and Christine Stückelberger and Granat from Switzerland going ahead to take the silver and gold respectively. Britain, though, won her first ever dressage medal, and interest in the sport took off.

SPONSORS: Franklin Mint Ltd

RESULTS
Team gold medal: Germany
Silver medal: Switzerland
Bronze medal: USSR

Individual gold medal: Granat with Christine Stückelberger for Switzerland
Silver medal: Slibowitz with Dr Uwe Schulten-Baumer for Germany
Bronze medal: Dutch Courage with Jennie Loriston-Clarke for Great Britain

Freestyle: Feudal with Dr Uwe Schulten-Baumer for Germany

1979

Franklin Mint had done their part for dressage and had launched Britain into the international scene as a major stage for the sport. A new sponsor was found in Inchcape plc, which backed the 1979 show through its subsidiary Toyota (GB) Ltd. It was the interest of the late Earl and the Countess of Inchcape that led to this vital support.

The feature of this show was that it included the first staging of an international freestyle to music, the competition that was to change the face of dressage.

It was the popular Canadian rider Cindy Neale (now Ishoy), who had spent years training in Europe with Willi Schultheiss, who came out on top.

SPONSORS: Toyota (GB) Ltd

RESULTS
Prix St Georges and Intermédiaire I: Equus with Cindy Neale (Ishoy) for Canada

Intermédiaire II: Amon with Annemarie Sanders-Keijzer for the Netherlands

Intermédiaire Freestyle: Tristan with Tilmann Meyer zu Erpen for Germany

Grand Prix and Freestyle to Music: Martyr with Cindy Neale (Ishoy) for Canada

1980

This was an Olympic year and there was a good boost to British morale when Jennie Loriston-Clarke and Dutch Courage beat the top German professional Georg Theodorescu on Cleopatra for the home country's first victory at Goodwood.

They managed a hat-trick, culminating in the first British victory in the Grand Prix Special. Also qualifying for this class was the future star for Germany, Monica Theodorescu, who was only seventeen years.

In this second running of a musical freestyle, ice-skater Robin Cousins was asked to assess the riders' interpretation of the music. His winner was Sarah Whitmore on Dutchman, a well-deserved success as she had ensured her music matched her horse's paces by getting it recorded by a local band.

SPONSORS: Toyota (GB) Ltd

RESULTS
Grand Prix and FEI Grand Prix Special and Intermédiaire II: Dutch Courage with Jennie Loriston-Clarke for Great Britain

Freestyle to Music: Asamaryu with Osamu Nakamata for Japan

Intermédiaire I: Phidias with Georg Theodorescu for Germany

Prix St Georges: Equus with Cindy Neale (now Ishoy) for Canada

1980 Dressage Festival

The invasion of Afghanistan by the Soviet Union led to worldwide protest, and riders were among the first to make the biggest sacrifice they could think of and refuse to compete at an Olympics which were to be staged in Moscow. Alternative Olympics, called Festivals, were laid on for each discipline at the last moment, and Goodwood, with its great reputation for organisation, was selected to stage the dressage at just ten weeks' notice.

The only rider of note, other than the Russians, to go to Moscow was the reigning European Champion Sissy Theurer from Austria. She won a rather meaningless individual gold medal as all the best riders went to Goodwood, where eleven nations were represented. Inchcape plc were the main sponsors, the Government gave financial support and another arena was put down. Mrs Thatcher, the Prime Minister, made a very rare appearance at a sporting event to thank the British Equestrian Federation for not going to Moscow.

The gold medals went as they had at the World Championships, the team going to Germany and the individual to that remarkable partnership of Christine Stückelberger and Granat.

SPONSORS: Inchcape plc

RESULTS
Prix St Georges and Intermédiaire I:
Turmalin with Christine Stückelberger for Switzerland

Intermédiaire II: Galapagos with Gabriela Grillo for Germany

Team gold medal: Germany
Silver medal: Switzerland
Bronze medal: Denmark
Britain – 6th

Individual gold medal: Granat with Christine Stückelberger for Switzerland
Silver medal: Slibowitz with Dr Uwe Schulten-Baumer for Germany
Bronze medal: Ahlerich with Dr Reiner Klimke for Germany
Dutch Courage – 6th

The Countess of Inchcape presents the trophy for the Grand Prix Special to Jennie Lorriston-Clarke and Dutch Courage – 'Hearing the national anthem played for us was one of the big moments of my life.'

Freestyle to Music: Galapagos with Gabriela Grillo for Germany

Grand Prix Special, FEI Grand Prix and Team Competition: Granat with Christine Stückelberger for Switzerland

FEI Intermédiaire I, Individual and Team Competition and FEI Prix St Georges: Turmalin with Christine Stückelberger for Switzerland

1981

Show classes were introduced this year and there was another first for Goodwood – They started the Young Horse Class with the Potential Dressage Horse for four- and five-year-olds. Amongst the entries were three future internationals: Hans Christian, whom Dr Bechtolsheimer was to buy; Dutch Gold with Jennie Loriston-Clarke; and Prince Consort with Diana Mason. This class was new to Britain and was aiming at the double purpose of being a good introduction to show-ring excitements for young horses and also as an aid to would-be dressage buyers as to what the experts believe are the right points to look for in a dressage horse. Mrs Jane Whiteley and Mrs Sheila Inderwick were the experts.

Merle Park CBE, the prima ballerina, was asked to judge the artistic quality of expression and movement in interpreting the music for the music freestyle. Her winner was Dutch Courage.

The straight dressage was won by the partnership which was to take over from Stückelberger and Granat: Ahlerich and Dr Reiner Klimke. After their victory at Goodwood they went on to win the 1982 World Championship, the 1984 Olympic golds in the team and individually, and the 1985 European Championship.

SPONSORS: Inchcape plc

RESULTS
Freestyle to Music: Carioca with Dominique d'Esmé for France

Prix St Georges and Intermédiaire I: Leon with Manfred Schmidtke for Germany

Grand Prix: Madras with Alexa Schulten-Baumer for Germany

Intermédiaire II: Amon with Annemarie Sanders-Keijzer for The Netherlands

Grand Prix and Special: Ahlerich with Dr Reiner Klimke for Germany

1982

In 1982 the Champions were another top combination: Dr Uwe Schulten-Baumer and Slibowitz, who had beaten Dutch Courage for the silver medal at the 1978 World Championships. The British, however, showed they had a special skill when it came to the musical freestyle and it was a British first, second and third when Dutch Courage won, followed by two new and important contributors to British dressage, the Bartle

siblings Jane and Christopher. They rode Pinocchio and Wily Trout respectively into third and second position, which was the start of many successes in music classes for this family.

SPONSORS: Inchcape plc

RESULTS
Prix St Georges: Rolling Stone with Manfred Schmidtke for Germany

Intermédiaire I: Patricia with Torben Olsen for Denmark

Intermédiaire II: Marzog with Anne-Grethe Jensen (Törnblad) for Denmark

Grand Prix and Special: Slibowitz with Dr Uwe Schulten-Baumer for Germany

Freestyle to Music: Dutch Courage with Jennie Loriston-Clarke for Great Britain

1983

For the tenth anniversary of the Goodwood International Competitions the FEI gave special dispensation for a team contest to be staged, which was won by Germany. Yet another great champion came to Goodwood in 1983. This was Marzog and Anne-Grethe Jensen (Törnblad) from Denmark, who went on to win the European Championships that year, the silver at the Olympics and the World title in 1976. Fifty-three show classes were held alongside the dressage.

The innovation of 1983 was the use of live commentary through headphones, which has done so much to make dressage more understandable. It was a huge success, remained a permanent feature of Goodwood, and many other shows followed suit both in this country and in Europe. It was later even used in the racecourse paddock and at the cricket matches at Goodwood. The man behind the idea was Chris Wright, a graphic designer.

The drama of that year was a freak hail

storm, when stones the size of golf balls so frightened the horse in the arena that it jumped out and galloped back to the stables. The show was brought to a standstill, and the freestyle postponed for over thirty-five minutes while the white covering of ice was cleared from the arena. When it was re-started Fay Crouch on Gilda tried to do her test while a stream of fire engines with sirens blazing raced to the house to pump out the flooded cellars. Then another terrible storm raged, with thunder, lightning and torrential rain. Even the English decided it was too much. The event was abandoned and Britain's David Hunt lost his first chance of an international victory as he was in the lead at the time.

SPONSORS: Inchcape plc

RESULTS
Prix St Georges: Candel with Hanneke Brök for the Netherlands

Intermédiaire I: Hava with Dominique d'Esmé for France

Intermédiaire II, Grand Prix and Special: Marzog with Anne-Grethe Jensen (Törnblad) for Denmark

The phenomenal hail storm in 1983, with stones the size of golf balls, which led to horses running away and the termination of the freestyle to music.

1984

Britain had a great show and a wonderful morale booster before the Olympics as Dutch Courage won the Grand Prix and the Special, but it was his final major victory as he was not right for the Olympics. David Hunt, then a professional, achieved his first international victory in the musical freestyle on Maple Zenith. Chris Bartle took the Intermédiaire II on Wily Trout.

SPONSORS: Inchcape plc

RESULTS
Prix St Georges and Intermédiaire I: Frenchman with Tutu Sohlberg for Finland

Intermédiaire II: Wily Trout with Chris Bartle for Great Britain

Grand Prix and Special: Dutch Courage with Jennie Loriston-Clarke for Great Britain

Freestyle to Music: Maple Zenith with David Hunt for Great Britain

1985

Clinique took over part of the sponsorship and the British Horse Society added further financial backing.

An exciting feature of 1985 was the start of the World Cup qualifiers, and it was fitting that the eventual winners of the finals (just beating Chris Bartle on Wily Trout), were also the winners of Goodwood's qualifier, Marzog and Anne-Grethe Jensen (Törnblad). This great Danish partnership won all the major classes.

Britain again managed some good results with Wily Trout winning the Intermédiaire II, and Sarah Whitmore's young stallion Troy making a promising international debut with placings in the Small Tour classes.

The most emotional event this championship was Dutch Courage's farewell, with support from many of his progeny and followed by a tea party on the Tapestry

Lawns of Goodwood House for his friends.

SPONSORS: Clinique, BHS

RESULTS
Prix St Georges: Vera Cruz with Juergen Koschel for Germany

Intermédiaire I: Mr X with Helen Aubert for the Netherlands

Intermédiaire II: Wily Trout with Chris Bartle for Great Britain

Grand Prix and World Cup Qualifier: Marzog with Anne-Grethe Jensen (Törnblad) for Denmark

1986

Britain earned the glory when Christopher Bartle on Wily Trout won all the top straight tests, but had to be content with second place in the World Cup qualifier, being beaten by his sister, Jane Bartle on Pinocchio.

These great victories were to be Christopher Bartle and Wily Trout's swansong and the following year the pair returned for a retirement parade.

SPONSORS: Nashua, British Horse Society

RESULTS
Prix St Georges: Charmeur with Madeleine Winter for Germany

Intermédiaire I: Troy with Sarah Whitmore for Great Britain

S13: Dutch Gold with Jennie Loriston-Clarke for Great Britain

Intermédiaire Freestyle: Hava with Dominique d'Esmé for France

Grand Prix and SII: Chris Bartle with Wily Trout for Great Britain

Nashua World Cup Qualifier: Jane Bartle (Wilson) with Pinocchio for Great Britain

Jane Bartle (Wilson) and Pinocchio, winners of the World Cup qualifier in 1986.

1987

Polly Peck stepped in to sponsor the first European Championships to be staged in Britain. A memorial service was held in the chapel of Goodwood House for Colonel Anthony Crossley, who had written up every one of the Goodwood international shows in *Horse and Hound*. Also, Wily Trout made his retirement parade.

SPONSORS: Polly Peck plc

RESULTS
Prix St Georges: Catherston Dutch Bid with Jennie Loriston-Clarke for Great Britain

Intermédiaire I: Maritim with Margit Otto-Crépin for France

Intermédiaire II: Courage with Ann-Kathrin Linsenhoff for Germany

Freestyle to Music: Dutch Gold with Jennie Loriston-Clarke for Great Britain

Team gold medal: Germany
Silver medal: Switzerland
Bronze medal: Netherlands

Individual gold medal: Corlandus with
Margit Otto-Crépin for France
Silver medal: Courage with Ann-Kathrin
Linsenhoff for Germany
Bronze medal: Ideaal with Jo Hinnemann
for Germany.

1988

Polly Peck continued their sponsorship. The
FEI allowed an unofficial team event.
France managed to beat the Germans in this
with the help of their great champion
Margit Otto-Crépin and Corlandus, who
won at Goodwood before going on to take
the Olympic individual silver medal.

In the German team was a seventeen-
year-old making her international debut on
Weingart, owned by her trainer, Dr Uwe
Schulten-Baumer. The young girl was
Isabell Werth, who went on to help
Germany win the team gold at that year's
Young Riders' Championships, and the following year became the youngest member of
the senior team when the Germans again
won the team gold at Luxembourg. Two
years later she herself won the European
individual title.

SPONSORS: Polly Peck plc

RESULTS
Prix St Georges and Intermédiaire I:
Winzlow with Madeleine Winter for
Germany

Intermédiaire II: My Way with Jenny
Erikson for Finland

Nashua World Cup Qualifier: Nektar
with Karin Rehbein for Germany

Grand Prix and Grand Prix Special:
Corlandus with Margit Otto-Crépin for
France

1989

In 1989 the style of Goodwood changed as
Hermés took over the sponsorship and
turned Goodwood into a great social occasion, inviting many who knew nothing
about dressage to come and watch and enjoy
some superlative Hermés hospitality. There
were plenty of parties and Goodwood
acquired a rather fashionable air with plenty
of coverage in the glossy magazines. It was
somewhat appropriate that the leading rider
was French: Margit Otto-Crépin took the
Goodwood Championship for the third
time. Britain earned some glory when Lady
Joicey took the Intermédiaire II on Aconto:
and future silver medallists for Britain, Laura
Shewen (Fry), still a Young Rider, and Quarryman, came fifth in the Intermédiaire I.

SPONSORS: Hermés

RESULTS
Prix St Georges and Intermédiaire I:
Ushin with Jeanette Haazen for the
Netherlands

Intermédiaire II: Aconto with Lady Joicey
for Great Britain

Nashua World Cup Qualifier: Supermax
Ravel with Anne-Grethe Törnblad
(Jensen) for Denmark

Grand Prix and Special: Corlandus with
Margit Otto-Crépin for France

1990

Hermés again added much glamour to the
event but this time handed their
Championship to a young German, Markus
Tecklenborg. Britain won plenty of the
honours as Anni MacDonald Hall filled the
runner-up spot in the Grand Prix and
Special on Floriano. Dane Rawlins took the
Intermédiaire II on Horsted Bright Spark,
and Jennie Loriston-Clarke won the Volvo
World Cup Qualifier on Dutch Gold, with
Diana Mason on Prince Consort the runner-

up. There was also a new event at this show for Young Riders, and the winner, Joanna Jackson, won a training scholarship which enabled her to go to Vienna.

Tanya Larrigan's Salute, member of several British teams, made a farewell following a walk which raised money for the Mark Davies Injured Riders' Fund.

SPONSORS: Hermés, Volvo

RESULTS
Prix St Georges and Intermédiaire I: Preacher Man with Markus Tecklenborg for Germany
Intermédiaire II: Horsted Bright Spark with Dane Rawlins for Great Britain

Grand Prix and Special: Franklin with Markus Tecklenborg for Germany

Volvo World Cup Qualifier: Dutch Gold with Jennie Loriston-Clarke for Great Britain

Lady Joicey.

1991

Recession reduced the extravagance of the Hermés entertainments but they remained the major sponsors alongside the British Horse Society and Volvo.

There was an Italian winner this year, as Pia Laus was the Champion on her stallion Adrett, with the European Champion of 1991, Isabell Werth, the runner-up in both classes.

SPONSORS: Hermés, BHS, Volvo

RESULTS
Prix St Georges: Windsor with Jeanette Haazen for the Netherlands

Intermédiaire I: Liebenberg with Pia Laus for Italy

Intermédiaire II: Olifant Charrière with Serge Cornut for France

Volvo World Cup Qualifier: Dutch Gold with Jennie Loriston-Clarke for Great Britain

Grand Prix and Special: Adrett and Pia Laus for Italy

1992

The need to qualify for the Olympics led to huge entries with fifty-six competitors in the Grand Prix, necessitating a division into two classes. Once again Adrett was a winner, and Carol Lavell took the second class on Gifted to become the first-ever winners for the USA in Britain. The honours were spread around the numerous countries represented, with Holland taking first and second in the championship event, the Special, with Montreux and Annemarie Sanders-Keijzer winning, and Olympic Larius and Ellen Bontje the runners-up. Britain had some good results with Carl Hester and Giorgione coming third in the Special and Virtu with Emile Faurie fourth.

The young stallion Olympic Cocktail excelled in the Volvo World Cup qualifier

The 1991 and 1993 European Champion Isabell Werth made her international debut at Goodwood when she was seventeen. Here she is rewarding her partner, Weingart.

to win with Anky van Grunsven for The Netherlands. Britain's greatest success was in the Small Tour with Joanna Jackson, in her first year out of Young Riders, winning on Mester Mouse.

Sponsors: Hermés, Volvo, K-Group

Results

Hermés Young Rider Scholarship: Giovanni with Lucy Farrer

Intermédiaire I and Prix St Georges: Mester Mouse with Joanna Jackson for Great Britain

Volvo World Cup Qualifier: Anky van Grunsven with Olympic Cocktail for the Netherlands

Grand Prix: Gifted with Carol Lavell for USA

Grand Prix: Adrett with Pia Laus for Italy

Grand Prix Special: Montreux with Annemarie Sanders-Keijzer for the Netherlands

1993

This was Goodwood's twenty-first year. When the overall sponsors bowed out, private individuals came to the rescue and funded this final event, James and Audrey Hartnett being the main benefactors.

Once again, massive entries entailed dividing the Grand Prix class into two sections. Canada earned her second Goodwood Championship with Christilot Boylen taking the title. In Giorgione's last ride with Carl Hester he was an impressive third in the Special. Emile Faurie earned his highest ever score in a Grand Prix.

Emile Faurie on the Russian stallion Olympus, a graded British Sports Horse, competing at Goodwood in 1993.

David Hunt on Maple Zenith, who won at the Goodwood International and were National Champions.

SPONSORS: Volvo and private individuals

RESULTS
British International Trainers' Young Riders: Pablo Picasso with Fiona Bigwood

Prix St Georges: Duphar with Frank Lamontagne for Germany

Intermédiaire I: Olympic Barbria with Tineke Bartels for the Netherlands

Grand Prix and Volvo World Cup Qualifier: Andiamo with Sven Rothenberger for Germany

Grand Prix and Special: Biraldo with Christilot Boylen for Canada

NATIONAL CHAMPIONS AT GOODWOOD

Jennie Loriston-Clarke 1981-1982
Jane Bartle-Wilson 1983
Christopher Bartle 1984-1985
Jane Bartle-Wilson 1986
Tricia Gardiner 1987

1988 David Hunt
1989 Diana Mason
1990 Anni MacDonald Hall
1991 Laura Fry
1992 Laura Fry

1993 Emile Faurie